Church Beyond Walls

Church Beyond Walls

Martin Poole

CANTERBURY
PRESS
Norwich

© Martin Poole 2023

Published in 2023 by Canterbury Press
Editorial office
3rd Floor, Invicta House,
108–114 Golden Lane,
London EC1Y 0TG, UK
www.canterburypress.co.uk

Canterbury Press is an imprint of Hymns Ancient & Modern Ltd
(a registered charity)

H
Y   Ancient
M
N   &Modern
S

Hymns Ancient & Modern® is a registered trademark of
Hymns Ancient & Modern Ltd
13A Hellesdon Park Road, Norwich,
Norfolk NR6 5DR, UK

British Library Cataloguing in Publication data

A catalogue record for this book is available
from the British Library

978-1-78622-482-8

Typeset by Regent Typesetting
Printed and bound in Great Britain by
CPI Group (UK) Ltd

Contents

Acknowledgements

None of the activities described in this book were achieved alone. Over the years hundreds of different people have been involved in helping to generate ideas, create art, steward events, give out flyers and countless other tasks that go to make up successful artistic events. There has always been a small core team of half a dozen or so close co-conspirators that has evolved and changed over the years as people have drifted in and out of involvement, but the one constant has been my presence to steer, cajole, administrate, irritate and co-create. There are too many to name but they know who they are and I am eternally grateful for their friendship, companionship and forbearance in this adventure of spirituality and creativity. The other constant has been the amazing support of my wife and family, who have put up with me turning our kitchen into a mulled-wine factory every December, saved the day when I've realized I've forgotten something, helped to make some of my crazier dreams come true and brought me back to reality when I've been too heavenly minded to be any earthly good. I could not have achieved any of this without the help of my children Billy, Esther and Amy and the constant love and support of my wife Sally.

Scripture quotations

Foreword

'The steps of the ladders are different heights ... ugh', my parishioner Amy proclaimed as I walked into a crumbling Denver church on the second Sunday of Advent in 2009. She wasn't wrong.

When we had decided to make a huge Advent calendar out of cigar boxes to be displayed on planks of wood, which we believed would lay flat on the steps of ladders without a problem, we had failed to consider that, say, the sixth step on each ladder would not necessarily be the same height.

But it was nothing an old hymnal propped under the left side of each plank wouldn't remedy.

When folks meandered into church, they were invited to lift the lid of each of the seven cigar boxes perched on their makeshift shelves and see what lay inside. One Reebok box had been plastered inside with sheet music. On the left, the notation for 'O Come Emmanuel' along with an ultrasound picture of a baby in utero, on the right, 'Joy to the world' and a photo of a newborn. The box next to it had been painted entirely black inside and out, with a tiny single light inside and 'A light shines in the darkness, and the darkness has not overcome it' printed on a slim strip of white paper and pasted to the back.

Our inspiration for creating a community Advent Calendar is clear: Revd Martin Poole of Beach Hut Advent Calendar fame.

The fact is, it would never have dawned on me to make a community art project in the form of an Advent calendar. But the idea needn't have dawned on me – because it dawned on Martin, and the Christian faith has always spread in its expansiveness and creativity from one community to the other, starting with

ix

the very first churches. Christians have always been each other's possibility models for what a lived faith can look like.

Oh wait. You guys eat pork and nothing bad has happened? Sweet. We're gonna let that rule go. The church in Jerusalem is collecting goods for orphans and widows? Never thought of that. We're totally gonna steal that idea. Hold on. Some Germans are just deciding to be Christian without taking orders from Rome? Genius. Let's go for it. Some group from a coastal city in England turned beach huts into a community Advent calendar? Amazing. Let's see what we could do that would be like that but probably not nearly as cool.

In each case, we Christians have reminded each other of this one thing that we tend not to remember we have, and that is: freedom. It is for freedom that Christ has set us free and for some reason, we tend to forget that. Like, all the time.

This means to me that Martin's creative spiritual projects are both completely innovative and completely in line with how Christian communities have influenced each other for generations. His community's public art installations which engage with matters of faith are not unlike artistic epistles to the church showing us what, where and with whom we *are free* to create. And then giving us permission to do just that.

Thanks be to God,
Revd Nadia Bolz-Weber
Advent 2022

Introduction

My name is Martin Poole. Currently, I am vicar of an Anglican church in Brighton on the south coast of England, but for most of my working life I've been a TV executive, travelling around the world creating brand identities and promotion campaigns for TV channels. I've also been an actor, butler, construction worker, receptionist, cleaner, youth volunteer and chaplain as well as a husband and father. For the purposes of this book, I'm the founder, principal curator and driving force behind Beyond, an arts and spirituality organization that has existed since 2008, producing creative events with a core of Christian spirituality.

Most of all, I'm a practitioner rather than a theoretician, and pretty much everything I've ever done has been by gut instinct, especially when it comes to things of the church. This intuitive approach has taken me from windswept beaches in the dark evenings of winter to crowds of thousands united by hundreds of winding ribbons; from redundant churches, hammering nails into timber in the darkness, to upper rooms in pubs where the floor was covered in the word 'God'.

My instinctual passion for finding new ways to express the message of God breaking into our lives has taken me on an amazingly varied journey of artistic exploration, and this book is an attempt to reflect on that journey and draw out some principles that others might find helpful as they seek to make God known in their own unique context. This subjective approach is the only way I know to tell this story and if at times a flavour of 'look at how fantastic this is' creeps into it then I apologize in advance and ask for your understanding and forbearance. My purpose with this book is not to blow my own trumpet but to help others experience something of the wonder I have felt when encountering God this way, and to help the church move away from its shuttered existence in creaky old buildings to find a new language without words and outside walls.

For some this book will be a practical handbook, full of ideas and techniques that can be put into practice in your own situation. For others it will be a simple tale of lives transformed by the beauty and love that are found in a God who breaks into our lives in moments of epiphany and revelation. There was a moment of epiphany for me in the summer of 2013 which put this project into context and gave me a theological framework to begin talking about our experiences at Beyond which, up to that point, had been hard for me to explain.

The setting was not one that would naturally suggest itself as a place where God was likely to be revealed in a particularly startling and unusual way. I was attending the Transforming Worship Conference of the Church of England Liturgical Commission as they were interested in the work of Beyond and had invited me to run a workshop. I thought I would take the opportunity to attend the whole conference, fully expecting to spend a couple of days in a series of rather dull lectures about the best way to write an intercessory prayer or whether it was a good idea to use colloquial language when writing a new prayer book.

At the opening of the conference, I settled down with a couple of hundred earnest-looking souls, a large proportion of whom were wearing clerical collars, to listen to the introductory talk by a Roman Catholic priest who I'd never heard of and didn't have much interest in. Father Ed Foley was the Duns Scotus Professor of Spirituality and Professor of Liturgy and Music at the Catholic Theological Union in Chicago, where he also worked as a priest at Old St Patrick's Church.

His theme was 'Re-imagining λειτουργία (Leitourgia)'. As Greek was the subject that I completely flunked during my theological training, I wasn't expecting to understand much of this, and after my long drive to the uninspiring Midlands university where the conference was being held, I was ready to have a little nap. I thought this subject sounded like the perfect sedative for my non-academic mindset so I found the most comfortable seat I could and hoped that no one was disturbed if I began to snore.

But Ed is not an award-winning author and highly sought-after speaker for nothing. He is entertaining and engaging, with the ability to make extremely academic subjects come to life with his illustrations and explanations. Not only that, but he knows how to make good use of PowerPoint, surely a twenty-first-century gift of the Holy Spirit that is desperately lacking in most church leaders today.

He began with a careful examination of the translation of *leitourgia* from Greek into English. Generally, when people in church circles talk about the meaning of the word 'liturgy', they use the phrase 'the work of the people'. This comes about because *leitourgia* is a compound word formed from *laos*, 'the people' (the same word from which we get the term 'laity'), and *ergon*, 'work'. This has been shortened in discussion about church worship to 'the work of the people'.

But as the Greek word exists in its own right and has a meaning of its own, we don't need to break it into its constituent parts to understand it. It's a word that is used in Greek culture to describe public acts of service, usually through the action of a benefactor. Events such as the Olympic games or, in Roman culture, the gladiator battles in amphitheatres could be described as liturgy as they were put on for the general public by wealthy benefactors. So a better translation is to say that *leitourgia* is about 'work FOR the people', not OF the people. If we carry the analogy on further, we could say that the church acts as the benefactor in this arrangement and is providing a public service for the people.

That all sounds straightforward and is not a bad description of what happens in most church services, except for another factor that Fr Foley wanted us all to take notice of, and that's where he took the radical step of introducing Jesus to the conversation.

The trouble with Jesus is that whenever you look at his life and teaching, your preconceptions are almost always turned upside down and what you thought was the case almost always turns out not to be true, and so it is when looking at Jesus' view of people. When we look at those with whom Jesus shared table fellowship (the most intimate and meaningful form of interaction in his culture at the time), we find that he seemed to spend most, if not all, of his mealtimes with outsiders and outcasts. He had lots of time for those who were on the margins of society and with whom no respectable person would normally associate, let alone dine. Alongside that, he was positively scathing about church people, even to the point of being abusive, and spent hardly any time with them, especially when it came to sharing a meal.

Taking these two principles in tandem, we end up with a formula for liturgy which doesn't look very like a prayer book or even a church service. We end up saying that *leitourgia* is the work FOR the people and that those people are the ones on the margins who are not part of our club. True liturgy is miles away from being a set of sacred rituals and responses known only to the initiated few in the sanctity of their cathedrals and churches. True liturgy is something that stirs people outside the church through acts of public service in which we hope they will experience God.

As Ed Foley explained all this, accompanied by beautifully simple diagrams on the enormous screen behind him, I got quite emotional as I realized the truth of his words through my own experience. Years of struggling to explain to people what I was trying to achieve with crazy outdoor art projects and immersive theatre-style worship all fell into place as acts of pure artistic liturgy. Suddenly I had a theological framework to help me to understand and explain why this work was truly church, even though it looked nothing like any church that most people had any understanding of.

That lecture was one of the many epiphanies that you're going to hear about in this book because I believe that that's the ultimate goal of all worship: to create opportunities for epiphany. Church should be about generating circumstances, actions, activities and events that create a space where God can act, never dictating what this action might look like, but always opening up the possibility of revelation. That's the goal of every artistic event I've ever created and the activity that I believe we are all called to if we really want church to mean something in the twenty-first century.

A stony beach on the south coast of Great Britain at six o'clock on a cold, wet and windy night in December is hardly the place you might expect to encounter God. As the wind whistles in from the sea, words from the Gospel of John ring out, telling everyone that the true light that enlightens everyone was coming into the world. The assembled company symbolically enacts the breaking of light into the darkness by snapping and twisting multicoloured glowsticks, and the night air is filled with neon flashes of light, like hundreds of exclamation marks, punctuating these ancient words from 2,000 years ago.

This is liturgy in the public square using art, symbolic action, theatre, word and prayer. Liturgy that is not bound by buildings or books or sets of rules and regulations, but liturgy that engages with people's lives and connects with their souls; liturgy that is meaningful and powerful as both word and action through the medium of art.

This is the kind of event that Jesus, who spent most of his ministry on the seashore and in the market square, would have recognized. This is the kind of setting that the man who admitted that he had no place to lay his own head would have understood as an appropriate place to house the words of God. This is the kind of church, unbounded by stone walls, oak doors and ancient practices, that the twenty-first century needs. A church that doesn't seek to contain God in a straitjacket of rules and ritual, but which releases the gospel of love into the world through art and beauty, freedom and understanding.

The church of the twenty-first century and beyond needs to change radically if it is to survive and be at all relevant to modern society. It needs to burst out from behind its cloistered walls and stained-glass windows and create new acts of sacred encounter appropriate for the public square. It needs to throw off the robes and rituals that were invented hundreds of years ago and devise new forms and festivals that are relevant to a modern way of thinking and being.

This is the new face of liturgy and art for the public square that this book seeks to express and articulate as I tell stories of our experiences in this spiritual adventure.

I

Community Art

Where do ideas come from? It's one of the wonders of the human brain that we can imagine things that have never existed before and, if we have the energy and the willpower, that we can conjure them into existence. In this sense we are all creators and I believe that when we engage in any kind of creative act, we are reflecting something divine. God is the original creator and we are fashioned in the image of God and so we cannot help being creative ourselves. So ideas come from our God-given imagination and are therefore divine. You could say all ideas come from God.

This idea began with a whinge, a grumble to some friends about one of the rules of beach hut design imposed by Brighton and Hove council. We had recently become the proud co-owners of a space on Hove seafront where we were allowed to build a beach hut. There are a few rules to a project like this, as the hut has to conform to a certain set of dimensions. The main structure of it has to be painted with a particular set of colours; the only variation in colour that's allowed in the paint scheme is on the doors, where owners can be as creative or expressive as they like. But no matter how these doors are painted, they must open inwards so that there is no danger to any passing promenaders who might walk into a flapping door or be unexpectedly halted in their tracks by someone bursting out of their hut and slamming it in their face like a scene from a Laurel and Hardy film.

While this is all very well and good for health and safety, it's not very convenient for usage as it means that a significant portion of the internal space of these huts is reserved for the doors to swing into, thereby reducing the serviceable space inside the hut. Having just been through the whole process of building a hut, I was moaning about this design and saying how much easier it would be if the doors opened outwards and, spotting one of my children's advent calendars, I pointed to that and said, 'Just like the doors on an Advent Calendar'. An Advent calendar using beach huts! The idea was born! We could use beach huts ranged along Hove seafront to create a giant Advent calendar! This moment of divine inspiration sprang out of my discontent about rules and regulations and my propensity to whinge about almost anything. Watch out for those times when God turns even our complaining into something magnificent and remember that all ideas are God's gift to us as creations of the ultimate creator.

I've often quoted the saying attributed to Edison: 'Genius is I per cent inspiration and 99 per cent perspiration' (he was probably quoting an American academic called Kate Sanborn who delivered a series of lectures on the topic 'What is Genius' – as is so often the case, the woman is rarely the person credited with a statement like this and it is then attributed to a man!). Whoever said it first – it is a truism that having an idea is just the first step in a long road to the realization of that idea, and the road to implementation is a hard slog and takes a lot of stamina. So after the eureka moment of realizing that beach huts had doors and that we could connect these to an Advent theme, I began to plot how to make this happen.

The first task was to get some beach huts and their owners involved. There are 450 beach huts on Hove seafront and we only needed 24 to do all the days leading up to Christmas Eve. I thought that ought to be easy, so that summer I produced a little flyer:

Would you like to take part in an exciting new event
for Brighton & Hove?
We're looking for beach hut owners
who would like be part of a
BEACH HUT ADVENT CALENDAR
Throughout the month of December, we hope a series
of beach hut owners will prepare a seasonal display

in their hut and agree to open their doors to the public
for one day in the early evening.
If you are interested in taking part, please contact
Martin Poole on info@beyondchurch.co.uk.

I printed 450 of these and set out one afternoon to deliver one to
every hut. Most had the leaflet poked under their door or wedged
in a crack somewhere, but a few were open, their owners enjoy-
ing the sun, and handing them the leaflet started a conversation
about the idea, to mostly positive responses. Some even offered
on the spot to take part. It helps when you're doing something
like this to be able to wear a clerical collar, as more often than
not it promotes conversation, although there are always a few
who give you an immediate brush off, which often makes me
wonder what their past experience of Christians has been.

After a couple of weeks, I had received a few responses and
with the help of friends with beach huts reckoned there were
enough participants to make this work; a few people would
have to double up but that would be OK for the inaugural year.
As mentioned on the flyer, we would only ever have one hut
open each evening as it would be too much to expect the person
who opened on 1 December to come out again every night until
Christmas Eve. Right from the start, the concept was that the hut
owners would do their own art and some of the participants had
already impressed me with their creative credentials. I arranged
a little get-together for those who had shown interest and we
began to talk about ideas, times of opening and a possible theme
for the calendar. It was decided that Christmas carols was a
good broad theme that connected everyone to the Christmas
story (no Rudolf the Red Nosed Reindeer or Jingle Bells!), and it
gave everyone plenty of leeway to be creative. Timing was set for
opening from 5.30 to 6.30 p.m., late enough for it to be dark but
early enough that families could have some time at home after
school and still come out to enjoy the hut before young children
had to go to bed.

I had already decided that the Beyond team would look after
the last hut on Christmas Eve, but we needed to allocate all

the other dates in December and so I began a 'bidding' process with the volunteers around days and dates. Predictably, Fridays, Saturdays and Sundays were the most sought-after days and it was hard to persuade people to do a hut on a Monday, Tuesday or Wednesday, but eventually we managed to agree a timetable for the month. Alongside this, I also asked people to pick a carol from a pre-prepared list on a first-come, first-served basis, the most popular choices being 'Away in a Manger', 'Hark the Herald Angels Sing' and 'While Shepherds Watched their Flocks by Night'.

The next task was to publicize the event – it's no good doing all the work to organize something like this if no one knows about it. Time was getting a bit tight so as soon as all the dates had been agreed, I designed a two-sided A5 flyer with what I hoped was a striking night-time image of beach huts on the seafront, a description of the event on the back, along with the timetable of hut openings and a very rudimentary map to help people find the right hut on the right night. People don't realize that the distance from hut 1 to 450 is one and a half miles along Hove seafront, and I didn't want people to miss a hut because they'd gone to the wrong end and didn't have enough time to walk to the correct hut. This was another reason for only ever having one hut open each evening, so as to concentrate the audience at that one location. We rush printed 15,000 flyers because my wife had the genius idea of asking schools to allow flyers to be distributed via the children's book bags and I'd managed to get more than a dozen schools to agree to do this for us. Additionally, of course, we had all the churches in Brighton and Hove as locations for our flyers, and a number of community locations such as libraries and cafés had agreed to take them.

These days, of course, you would make much greater use of social media and we did set up website pages and a blog, but Facebook was only two years old in 2008 and not widely used. These days, we do almost everything online, which is quicker and better for the planet, although we need to ensure that we're not just talking to our own little echo chamber.

Alongside this blitz of paper, I also embarked on a PR campaign using every contact I could find in local media to talk about the event. Focusing on local radio and newspapers for an event like this is important as the aim with all publicity is to get people to come along and they're only likely to do that if they live nearby. Local media are also usually easier to talk to about a story like this than national media, and a lot more immediately responsive and straightforward to deal with.

Keeping the local focus in mind, I also produced a series of posters using the flyers and got agreement from every beach hut owner taking part to post one of these on their beach hut door with an 'open here' message pointing to the date that that particular hut would be open. It's surprising how many people go out for a sunset walk along the Hove seafront, even in the winter, and of course these people are pretty likely to be interested in turning up for the hut openings as they're already the type of person who goes out at that time anyway.

The final piece of the logistical puzzle to put together was refreshments. As an incentive for people to come along, we decided to offer free mince pies and mulled wine, and so I set about working out how to do this on Hove seafront with no power and very little light. A fold-up picnic table was purchased, along with a pump-action hotel-style vacuum flask to hold 3 litres of hot liquid. The local supermarket was almost cleaned out of their early supply of mince pies as I bought a car-boot-full of them. A jumbo battery pack was ordered online, complete with a set of pedals that, it was claimed, could be used to charge it if the battery went flat. A quick visit to the pound store (an absolutely essential resource for any kind of creative worship) yielded a haul of cheap battery-powered Christmas lights and batteries. All of this was stored in the back of our car, which became Advent Calendar HQ for the month of December. A friend supplied me with a recipe for mulled wine, which was brewed up on the early afternoon of the first hut opening, creating what became a Christmas tradition in our house of wonderful aromas every day throughout the month, permeating everything we did for the next 11 Decembers.

And so to the opening ...

After a three-month build up and a lot of work, the very first Advent Beach Hut opened its doors (or rather was unveiled – due to the aforementioned doors opening inwards it was never possible to have an actual 'opening'), themed on the carol 'Mary's Boy Child'. It turned out that playing the carol on a little tape recorder was the only reference we had to the theme, as the hut decoration consisted of a gas heater pumping out a warm red glow, a couple of plinths with a flower display on one and an apple in a bowl on the other, some candles in the hut and a candelabra set on a dining table next to some jolly garden gnomes!

This was my first lesson in accepting whatever interpretation an individual may bring to their creative endeavours for an event like this. For something like this to be a true community event, it's important that people are allowed to express themselves in the way they see fit. Sometimes this may not accord with your own taste or creative standard but often this will provide some insight into the themes of Advent and Christmas that are not 'orthodox' but are genuinely felt and which those of us in the church should take notice of.

What we did have that night was an amazingly clear sky and an unusual conjunction of Venus and Jupiter right next to a crescent moon, which was so extraordinary that people were stopping their cars to see this as they drove along the seafront. We also had a pleasing first-night turnout of about 60 people, meaning that I rapidly had to revise my plans for catering each night!

The following night we headed to a different hut and 'O Little Town of Bethlehem', which began a common theme that often cropped up as part of the Beach Hut Advent Calendar – a nativity scene. In this case it came complete with light-up stars in the ceiling of the hut, straw on the floor and children from the family who owned the hut dressed up as an Angel, Joseph and Mary, who carried with her a baby Jesus in a Moses basket.

Now, the purists in church circles might baulk at this, as of course baby Jesus isn't born until Christmas Day and in this case, he was a full 23 days premature; but a nativity scene without a baby Jesus doesn't look right and this can often be the start of an interesting conversation about Christmas timing. One comment

I received after a particularly beautiful nativity hut was that it made the people who came along realize that 'This child is for life, not just for Christmas.' I remember one night having a conversation with a gentleman at one of the huts who thought that there was too much Jesus in the Beach Hut Advent Calendar, to which I pointed out that we were heading towards Christ-mas and that the clue was in the name of the festival, something that had never occurred to him!

The fact is, beach huts are an ideal setting for a nativity as they so perfectly reflect what we think the stable would have looked like in first-century Bethlehem. The Beach Hut Advent Calendar has given many children a chance to dress up as an angel or Mary or Joseph or even as a donkey or a sheep, which I hope is something they will remember for the rest of their lives. Over the years people have been extremely creative with their beach hut nativity scenes as they've found ingenious ways to mount shining stars on poles above their hut, swathed the floors of their huts in straw, created smells that you might find in a stable and filled them with animals, both real and pretend.

One particular hut that focused on animals in a unique and inspirational way took 'While Shepherds Watched Their Flocks by Night' as their carol. I make a point of never asking beforehand what the hut owner proposes to do as I don't want to interfere with their idea and I liked discovering the art as a surprise, in the same way as an advent calendar at home when you never know what the image is going to be behind the door until you open it. This night I turned up to find that the hut owner had carpeted the floor of the hut with fake grass and had painted the walls and ceiling dark blue to enhance the strings of starry lights that were hung across this night sky. But the most impressive feature was the huge flock of miniature sheep which grazed happily under the watchful eye of some shepherds and an angel.

Each sheep was an oblong ball of fluffy cotton wool about the size of my hand with a cute little face and ears made of black card stuck on the front. So simple and yet brilliantly effective, and quite breathtaking in its execution. A row of tealights in glass jars ranged along the front of the hut, giving a beautiful

warm light, and we had a cello player accompanying us play-ing Christmas carols. This was a magical evening that brought a sense of holy awe to all who came along; it was so different from the garish lights and blaring Christmas music that is the usual experience of Christmas for most people. Among the hundred or so visitors that night were some Japanese students who had come to Brighton to learn English, and I had an interesting time explaining to them what an Advent Calendar was, how it related to Christmas and what this season meant to me as a Christian. There were many times to have conversations like this over the 11 years that we ran this event.

Early on in this first-ever Beach Hut Advent Calendar I began to get requests from various media to cover the event, which is an enormous privilege and of course great publicity but also quite tricky to manage. The best way to get good coverage is to make it as easy as possible for them to get a good story. Where television news is involved, this often means getting more than one hut for them to film, which is difficult as most huts only get set up on the day. One of the early huts in this first year was my own and I had decided to do something with light and lasers following an Advent event we'd run with the artist Chris Levine (see Chapter 7). I could set this up ahead of my actual day in the calendar and I knew this would make good TV but that it would have to be filmed in the dark and the reporter and crew wanted to come along mid-afternoon. The hut being opened the night the crew were there was owned by one of our team, who was happy to talk about the real meaning of Christmas being about love, as their carol was 'Love Came Down at Christmas', and I was also able to get the next hut owner to set hers up early so that there were three huts for the crew to feature as part of their story.

The thing that has always amazed me is how ready the media are to allow us to talk about the reasons behind what we're doing rather than just promote the activity itself. Over the years in countless interviews about this event on TV, radio and in print, I've always been able to talk about the different themes of Advent, whether it be about expectation for the coming of Christ into our lives or the need we all have for light in the darkness. This media coverage then becomes an extension of the event and its message, reaching a much wider audience than those who simply turn up on the night. We often only think of the media as a conduit to publicize our event but it is possible to include a gospel message as part of a media interview; after all, the medium is the message according to Marshall McLuhan, so let's use it as such.

Having said that, the focus should always be on those who turn up on the night as that is the heart of the project, the person-to-person message of Advent and Christmas. That is never more important than at the final hut on Christmas Eve, which was always reserved as a Beyond night and became a memorable part of Christmas tradition for so many families. That first year, the numbers attending day by day gradually grew from the 60 or so at the first night to over a hundred most evenings, but little could we have guessed at the explosion of people in attendance on Christmas Eve.

My wife took the creative reins that night as she had a vision for a hut themed on the carol 'We Three Kings'. Once again, to church purists this is an Epiphany carol and shouldn't be sung until 6 January, but it usually crops up in church carol services and is a great favourite to be sung at this time of year. Sally had a vision of three wise men on stilts stepping out of the hut while we all joined in with the song. I pointed out this was a bit impractical as a hut was only 2 metres high and the doorway even lower. Nevertheless, this dream remained in the back of our minds as she set about decorating the hut with a gold backdrop showcasing three carved wooden magi we had purchased from a local art shop. On the night we planned to burn frankincense and offer people a blessing with myrrh oil so that all three of the gifts in the story were represented as part of the installation.

Two days before Christmas Eve I was doing some last-minute gift shopping and noticed three guys busking outside Brighton's main shopping centre, and they were on stilts! Between songs I shouted up to them to ask if they were free on Christmas Eve and if they would like to earn £100. They replied yes and we had a quick exchange of phone numbers and made arrangements for their debut as the fabled wise men.

Unfortunately, on the night it turned out they were not quite as wise as I had hoped – 5.30 p.m. came and went with no sign of them, and at 5.45 I got a frantic phone call saying they had gone to the wrong part of the beach and were all dressed up and strapped into their stilts, which severely limited their ability to walk long distances. Fortunately, a friend who was helping had his estate car parked nearby and raced off to find them. By putting the seats down the three musicians were able to lay down in the back of the car, complete with stilts, and were driven to a spot near to our hut.

The upshot of this was that they eventually arrived at 6 p.m., right in the middle of the event, striding towards us from the east, singing and playing 'We Three Kings' at the top of their voices – it was magical. We estimate more than 250 people turned up that night to enjoy mulled wine, mince pies, roast chestnuts and carol singing. Shortly after the wise men arrived, I hopped up onto a box and at the top of my voice read the story of the magi arriving to worship the holy child, before leading a rousing chorus of the carol. I then blessed the crowd and let them know that I would be offering individual blessings with myrrh oil a hundred yards away from the crowds, under one of the beach-front street lights. No sooner had I taken up my position than a long queue of people formed to receive a blessing. As each person stepped up, I dipped my thumb in the oil and marked the sign of the cross on their forehead with the words, 'May the blessing of the Christ child be yours this Christmas.' One of the last people to come forward was a middle-aged woman whose face was streaked with tears. She whispered to me that she had just been diagnosed with cancer and wanted God to give her strength for whatever was to come. The whole nine months of preparation and hard work in making this God-given idea come to fruition was worth it for that one moment.

Over the years that we ran this event there were many memorable and meaningful nights like this.

One year the theme was angels, and I turned up one night to find a hut completely lined with silver foil, a ten-year-old boy dressed as an astronaut, and lots of tiny stars and satellites made from sewing-machine bobbins hanging by nylon threads. I asked the hut artist to talk me through her thinking on this and she

told me how she had been reading up on angels and realized that they are often messengers from God. This led her to think about how we message each other today, digitally from where we are to anywhere in the world, and how the wonders of modern technology mean that we have the divine power of angels as we can message anyone, anywhere at any time, and that's what her hut represented.

Another hut owner was a contemporary dancer. She used the theme of angels to fill the floor of her hut knee-deep in feathers and she and a partner choreographed a 15-minute dance to the k.d. lang track 'Calling All Angels'. In another year this same artist took the concept of journey as her inspiration for a fifties-style dance about travelling. She told me how she became aware that the Christmas story was full of journeys – Mary and Joseph to Bethlehem, the shepherds down from the hills to the stable, the wise men across many lands from the East to worship the king – and she wanted to reflect this in a journey of life that was both practical and spiritual.

One of the artists who got involved right from the beginning was Janette, who late in life had started to paint and had developed a fascination with the virgin Mary. Each year she would produce some new paintings of her that she would exhibit in a friend's hut, using it as a little art gallery. She told me that she found God through her painting and the art had a spiritual significance for her. In 2012 she wasn't feeling too well the night of her hut opening but still managed to put up her paintings with the help of her husband, although she spent most of the time that evening sitting in their car sheltering from the weather. Shortly after Christmas I got the news that she'd been diagnosed with terminal cancer and in August of that year I had the privilege of conducting her funeral. But that wasn't the end of her involvement with the Beach Hut Advent Calendar. That December her husband asked if he could open the hut that she had always used for her art. He didn't claim to have any artistic gifts, but on the night, he produced a simple life-size image of an 18-year-old Janette from when they had first met, which stood in the doorway where previously her paintings of the virgin Mary had stood.

The hut that night became a vigil for her, and many friends and family came to pay their respect and to celebrate her life.

We had many memorable Christmas Eve huts and the crowds grew and grew, with many people treating this as the traditional beginning of their family Christmas.

One year I was introduced to the artist Jimmy Cauty, one-time member of KLF and co-artist/conspirator with Bill Drummond. He really wanted to do the Christmas Eve hut and his first idea was to fill it from floor to roof with discarded Christmas wrapping paper as a comment on the environmental waste of commercialized Christmas. I gently pointed out that we were a Christian organization and we'd like the Christmas Eve hut to have a spiritual theme if possible. He took that on board and said: 'OK, I want God in the Hut. A massive light, just visible through a crack in the doors, let's do that.'

So I set about the practical limitations of making this happen – once again 1 per cent inspiration, 99 per cent perspiration. You will recall that there is no power in the huts so I arranged to rent a generator. A TV producer friend offered to loan me a couple of high-power studio lights and a smoke machine, and on the day we set about installing all of this in the hut, along with a PA that Jimmy had supplied to play a soundtrack that he'd put together. The doors to the hut were closed and at 5.30 p.m. they opened a couple of inches to reveal a blast of intense white light and whisps of smoke emanating from inside. At the same time Jimmy's 'soundtrack' began, which was a continuous low rumble that went on for the whole hour we were open. People began arriving and stood watching this hut that felt as if it was about to take off into the night like some kind of space rocket, but never did. The constant question that evening was, 'What's going to happen?' to which the reply was, 'This is Advent, the season of expectation for what is going to happen on Christmas Day.'

Once again at 6 p.m. I hopped up on a box, this time with a PA and microphone to help me be heard over the 500 or so people who had assembled. Volunteers moved around the crowd distributing glowsticks and I began to read the opening of the

Gospel of John. I got to 'The true light that gives light to every-one was coming into the world', and we moved on to 'The Word became a human being. He made his home with us. We have seen his glory. It is the glory of the One and Only, who came from the Father. And the Word was full of grace and truth' (John 1.9, 14 NIrV).

At this point I stopped and asked everyone to lift their glow-sticks above their heads and to break light with me. The crowd was absolutely silent except for the cracking of the sticks being broken and the outbreak of different-coloured lights that followed. I thanked the throng for coming out and invited them to take these glowsticks home as a sign that Jesus, the light of the world, was coming to their homes this Christmas. This became a regular ritual that we practised most Christmas Eves as the final hut opening of the Beach Hut Advent Calendar. We rarely if ever used a formal liturgy as generally I like to respond to the moment in an appropriate way, any texts that we use at any point during the Beach Hut Advent Calendar usually came straight from the Bible.

This spark of an idea that grew from me complaining about the design of a beach hut resulted in 11 years of art installations on

Hove seafront, 264 opportunities for epiphany as widely diverse individuals and groups of people exercised the divine gift of creativity. But the impact of this one idea isn't limited to this one place and time: there have been spin-off events in other places around the UK and around the world that have inspired people to be creative around the themes of Advent and Christmas.

You don't need a beach or a beach hut to run a community art Advent event, you just need a series of locations or even just one.

If you're nowhere near a beach you could use garages as your nightly location for an art installation. This is what the Oxted Adventure did, creating a trail around various homes in the town. The advantage of this is that electricity is readily available and garages are usually slightly more protected from the elements than a beach hut on a windy strand in the middle of December! It also means that neighbours get to meet each other and a sense of community develops around the planning and implementation of this, as well as during the event itself.

Others have used shop windows as the basis for a local Advent trail – see the chapter on Retail Spirituality for more practical advice on running something with traders. It's not even necessary to have a number of different locations; some churches have set up one location and had a different art event happening in that one place each night, so that the surprise is not about finding the venue but about the content that is going to be in it. This could be a beach hut, as was the case in Bridlington, where the council gave a church group a hut to use for the whole of December, or it could be a temporary shed built on a village green or a horse box installed in a churchyard for the whole month. It could even be a church or perhaps the lych-gate of a churchyard, although I'd always argue that there's more impact in taking these ideas out into public spaces.

Make sure you put aside some time to think about the best way to publicize your event. Social media is an easy and cheap way to let people know about something but be aware that this usually means you're only talking to your own little echo chamber. Actively look for ways to get the message out to groups that might not otherwise hear about your Advent calendar. Getting schools involved is a great way to get a ready-made audience for any particular night, especially early on in the month, as then lots of families will come out and will be aware that this on for the rest of December. Schools love to have a Christmas project to focus on in their Autumn term as a craft activity for children, and school choirs make an ideal focus for one evening and will engender the right kind of Christmas spirit.

I quickly realized that I was seeing some of the same people night after night and this led to the creation of a simple loyalty scheme, just like the ones that coffee shops offer when you visit more than once. I created a little rubber stamp and when people came, they could collect a stamp and whoever had the most stamps on Christmas Eve would win a prize. This could be a Christmas hamper, or a year's supply of chocolate or a family meal at a local restaurant, all items that businesses were happy to donate. Amazingly, over the years there were always a number of people who presented a card with 100 per cent attendance on Christmas Eve. These were people I had the privilege of getting to know over the course of 24 conversations, hearing about their lives and their own relationship with the themes of Advent or the Christmas story. For the final Beach Hut Advent Calendar in 2018 we produced a 24-piece jigsaw of one of the very first huts and gave out an individual piece every night to create a souvenir as a way of marking 11 years of this amazing event.

The key to getting people involved creatively is to make it easy for them. Give them a simple theme as a hook for their work, make it at a time that is convenient and take away all the worry about publicity and the logistics of refreshments and, if necessary, any practical arrangements. That way they can just focus on being creative. Many people say that they're not creative or don't have the artistic skill to produce something but as Picasso said, 'Every child is an artist. The problem is how to remain an artist when you grow up.' Remind those who have an understanding of church that we are fearfully and wonderfully made in the image of God our creator and that includes being creative in the same way that God is. Ultimately if a person wants to be involved but isn't confident about their artistic ability, partner them up with someone who is; we often had approaches from people who wanted their beach hut to be used, at the same time as having artists who wanted to be involved who didn't have a hut, and so we put them together to collaborate.

Remember above all to allow people to respond creatively in the way that they choose. This will result in some ideas that you would never have dreamt of as well as some that might make you a bit uncomfortable, but this becomes an opportunity to explore your own faith and the relationship between faith and creativity in your own life. Above all this is an activity where God can act and where the divine can break into people's lives in unexpected, inspirational and transformative ways. So have a go!

Things to consider

- Be open to God-given ideas anywhere and everywhere.
- Accept whatever artistic ideas others contribute; you might learn something about God through them.
- Be prepared to work to make your idea happen.
- Explain your ideas simply when trying to get wider involvement and volunteers.
- Schedule the event based on who you would like to attend and what time suits them.
- Pay attention to publicity beyond your own small demographic.
- Make all publicity clear and comprehensive.
- Create some kind of loyalty scheme so that people come back every night.
- Use local media to promote your event and cultivate relationships with them.
- People are prepared to give money for something they appreciate; donations often get a better response than making them pay.

2

Spiritual Trails

I've never been a great fan of guided tours; it's partly an aversion to being treated as part of a group, partly because I prefer to go my own way and to discover things for myself. I'm also quite impatient when exploring and like to move on at my own pace rather than wait for a guide to explain every last detail of whatever it is we're looking at. For that reason, I never take the audio guide in a museum or art exhibition even though I'm sure I miss out on details that would enhance my understanding of the visit. So it's ironic that I have spent time putting together trails for people that mimic this same format.

The idea for the Lent Trail came originally from an installation at the Beach Hut Advent Calendar. The hut owner in this case was a music producer and one year she chose 'Silent Night' as her theme carol and installed a silent disco in her hut for the evening. I had never come across this technology before and was fascinated by it. It consists of a simple wireless transmitter hooked up to a music source, an mp3 player or similar, and any number of sets of wireless headphones. She installed this set-up in her hut and provided two channels of music: one was a very meditative reflective channel playing versions of 'Silent Night', the other was a more upbeat rocking version of various Christmas carols.

I was fascinated by the technology and began to think about ways we might use it as part of some sort of trail. The first opportunity to do this was as part of the Greenbelt arts, faith and justice festival. The festival was taking place on an expansive open site and people often go for walks when the weather is pleasant, on top of the daily trudge back and forth to the campsite. I thought it

23

would be interesting to see if we could use this technology to create a walk that would add an audio element to the natural environment inherent in the site; we called this the Silent Pilgrimage.

The plan was that we would use the low range of the wireless connection to set up five 'broadcasting stations' that were far enough apart not to interfere with each other. Then a participant with a set of headphones could start at one end of the walk listening to one particular audio meditation and as they slowly walked along a set path this would morph into the second meditation and then the third, and so on. I managed to get hold of five transmitters and a set of headphones, and after some experimenting in a local field, worked out that if they were placed 100 metres apart then we could achieve the desired effect. Each transmitter would have a battery-powered mp3 player attached to it and the transmitters themselves could also be battery powered.

The next job was to get some audio and so I approached four alternative worship groups that I had come into contact with through Greenbelt previously and asked if each of them would be able to produce a five-minute audio meditation to go with the one that we would produce at Beyond.

They all agreed, and a couple of weeks before the festival I had five very different audio meditations in my possession. These included an ambient music track for the beginning, mixed with words read by the astronauts on Apollo 8 as they rounded the moon on Christmas Eve 1968, describing the beginning of the world from Genesis. There was a celebratory techno music track about resurrection including some of the liturgy to the Eucharist, a quiet track using notes from different-sized prayer bowls as a background to a song of breath and spirit featuring several different female voices. Another track was about the pressure to conform and the influence of commercialism in shaping our presentation of ourselves, featuring a multi-layered chorus of chanting male voices, and the whole piece finished with a poem of blessing whispered by an ethereal voice underscored by yet more techno music.

Each of these was loaded onto a separate cheap mp3 player and we were ready to go. I had scouted a location at one edge of the festival site where there was a long expanse of fence so that we could use fence posts 100 metres apart to attach our little installations of mp3 players and transmitters, and made arrangements with one of the venues to act as a pick-up point for the wireless headphones.

Once a day during the festival I would go along and change the batteries and check that the meditations were still playing on continuous loop, and we left the whole installation for people to engage with however they wanted. It was mainly a 'proof of concept' idea as the walk itself was a path in a straight line for 500 metres alongside a fence and wasn't that interesting. As I listen back to the meditations, I do wonder how people who took part would have felt walking along a green and pleasant piece of Cheltenham countryside listening to decidedly non-natural techno/rave audio or a recording of someone reciting 'gotta look nice, gotta look good' for five minutes and whether this would have enhanced the walk – I'm not sure!

My reflection on the trail afterwards, which to be honest was a sideshow for us as we had other preoccupations at the festival that year, including a 2.5-tonne ice sculpture, was that as well as the audio it needed to have more of a visual focus than just countryside. I had always thought that there ought to be a way to open people's eyes to the possibility of God being present in our ordinary everyday lives if only we were open to this, and that audio could help. I had experienced this myself on occasion without any particular prompting, suddenly being arrested by the colours on a poster that made me feel that being able to see colour was a divine gift, or noticing the shadow of a street sign that looked like a cross making me pause for a moment of prayer. I was convinced there could be a way to use audio to help people experience the world in a different way and to give divine meaning to places and objects that would otherwise be ignored. And so began the development of Lent Through the Lanes.

I'd already done one kind of trail through the Brighton Lanes (see Chapter 5) so had some experience of setting something like this up, but this had some constrictions that needed to be navigated around. The audio stations had to be far enough apart not to interfere with each other, but close enough so that there wasn't too big a gap in the audio for the pilgrim with the headphones. If possible, I wanted to use found imagery or iconography to highlight that there are things of God all around us if we simply look. I only had five transmitters so we could only have five locations, and we needed somewhere for people to be able to pick up headphones and a process for doing that which would ensure that they were returned.

Working creatively within a set of constrictions like this is often really helpful as it helps you to focus your ideas and they become more intense. People sometimes say that we need to 'think outside the box' or that there's a 'completely blank canvas', neither of which I find to be very helpful. Working inside a box makes you push against the boundaries and gives you a frame to work in. If you're having trouble coming up with an idea, give yourself some limitations and see how you can manoeuvre within those to produce something wonderful; it really makes you think.

I started from the premise that the project needed a base where people could pick up headphones that would be open most days, so that the trail could be walked by anyone at their convenience.

LENT THROUGH THE LANES

13TH MARCH - 24TH APRIL

I'd already worked with the Brighthelm Centre on the Easter Path so approached them for help and they very kindly agreed to host the event. I decided that each set of headphones should have some sort of deposit to ensure that they got returned and we set that at £20 as we figured most people would have a £20 note they would be happy to hand over for an hour or so.

Then began the process of finding or creating art that could be given some spiritual meaning by adding audio, and it made sense to begin with something close to Brighthelm. As I left the building, I came across a tree in their garden with decorations in it. It turned out that it had been planted in memory of those who had died of AIDS and the branches of the tree were decorated with the small red ribbons that are often found on the lapels of those who want to show their solidarity with that cause. These stood out against the starkness of the leafless tree, as this was March and all the trees were stripped of their leaves and had not yet come into bud. Location and artwork number one was right there on the doorstep, a great start.

I then began to scour the streets for the next location, knowing that I couldn't stray much more than 100 metres from the home base and also that a built-up area would make a difference to the distance that the wireless signal could be received. I circled around Brighthelm, gradually increasing the distance from my starting point, inspecting the shops and street furniture I was passing and making notes about anything that I thought might have some spiritual potential.

A couple of streets away I came across a tattoo parlour called Penetration. This had been in the back of my mind anyway as a possibility in relation to Jesus being pierced and crucified and I was delighted to discover that their window featured a sculpture of Jesus on a cross made out of recycled materials! It stood about 1.5 metres high and was made of reclaimed wood with a painted image of Jesus and the outline, his halo and the folds of his robe, all drawn with hundreds of multicoloured bottle tops. In the centre of the image was a sacred heart made from a heart-shaped scrap of wood that was emanating rays of light represented by rows of shiny buttons.

I went into the shop and spoke to the manager and it didn't take long to explain the idea, that it wouldn't take up any of their time or resources except for a little bit of electricity, and that potentially it could drive customers to them or at the very least encourage people who'd never consider a tattoo to look in their window! They readily agreed, and so having taken their card I promised to be in touch with more information nearer the time.

I had a vague idea that I wanted to head down towards the seafront at some point in the trail as I thought it would be good to get to the sea during the walk, and so I headed off in that direction once again on the lookout for potential spiritual locations. Nothing came to mind until I came out just in front of the famous Brighton Pavilion. It was a bit further than I had hoped but most of the walk from the tattoo shop was along open public gardens and so the wireless signal would probably carry quite well. I had stopped because this was the location of the Brighton civic war memorial featuring a number of different commemorations of the dead from various wars and conflicts over the last 100 years. This would do well for the third location as scripture has quite a lot to say about those who give up their lives for others, and all I'd need to do was find a base for the transmitter.

Continuing my walk towards the sea I arrived at the Brighton seafront and began walking westward until I came across the Kiss Wall. This is a 4-metre-high black aluminium plinth, reminiscent of the monolith in the film *2001: A Space Odyssey* except that this contained some imagery. Pierced through the aluminium are a series of portraits of six couples of various ages and genders, kissing. These are rendered in a dot matrix format, rather like low-resolution newsprint and looking similar to the giant pop-art paintings of Roy Lichtenstein. The images reveal themselves and change as you walk past the sculpture, depending on the light shining through it. It's an artwork celebrating equality, understanding and acceptance of all individuals and I was certain there would be a way for us to incorporate it into our trail.

I felt the final location for the trail would need to take participants back towards the beginning so that it was convenient to hand their headphones back and retrieve their £20 deposit. I headed inland directly towards Brighthelm and found myself walking past the Chapel Royal, which is the most central Anglican church in Brighton, and I felt certain that the priest there would be open to us putting something in one of the windows as he was a good friend. I liked the idea that among the found items of art that made up the content of most of the trail there would be something bespoke that we had created ourselves.

So, learning from the randomness of the Silent Pilgrimage audio, I began to explore with our team what audio we might use at each location. Fortunately, one of our group worked for a company that supplied and built audio facilities and was an experienced audio producer himself and so we knew that we could produce five audio tracks which would be thought-provoking and good quality. Alongside each of the audio tracks we would also produce a small card to go on display at each location to explain the project and to give some textual detail to the meditation in that particular location.

We decided that as the first location was a tree, we would focus on the tree of knowledge in the garden of Eden in Genesis 3 and the declaration by God that as a result of eating the forbidden fruit, Adam and Eve would now live lives of struggle and sweat and that they were made from dust and to dust they would return. I look back on this ten years later with the hindsight of education about equality, sexuality and inclusive language and think we might have chosen something different for this location today. As this tree was commemorating those who have died from AIDS, I would want now to go out of my way to avoid any suggestion that there is a connection with sin when discussing this issue. I know that at the time our intention was to highlight that death is part of the human condition for us all, but as I read the words of the sign we posted at this location I can see how it might be interpreted as describing those who died of AIDS as more sinful than the rest of us, something that I do not believe to be the case. One of the issues we need to be careful of when creating public work of this nature is to check our understanding with those who have personal experience so as to avoid insensitive interpretations.

The second location was easy as the activity of the shop and the artwork naturally lent themselves to words about Jesus being pierced for our sake and so I turned to Isaiah 53, words that are often thought to be prophetic of Christ's crucifixion. The description card for the window said:

This shop specializes in body piercing and tattooing. The artwork in the window is by a Brighton artist and depicts Christ on the cross made from recycled materials. For many people the words of the prophet Isaiah sum up very well the purpose of Jesus' crucifixion.

'He took our pain and bore our suffering, yet we considered him punished by God, stricken by him, and afflicted. But he was pierced for our transgressions, he was crushed for our iniquities; the punishment that brought us peace was on him, and by his wounds we are healed.' Isaiah 53.4–5 (NIV)

Similarly, the war memorial already dictated the content that we might use for the meditation as we already had Jesus' words about loving one another and the greatest love being by those who lay down their lives for their friends. We chose to pair this with verses from 1 John 3: 'This is how we know what love is: Jesus Christ laid down his life for us. And we ought to lay down our lives for our brothers and sisters. Let us not love with words or speech but with actions and in truth' 1 John 3.16, 18 (NIV).

Next came the Kiss Wall and we drew on experience gained from developing our own version of a Tenebrae service on Holy Saturday the year before this (see Chapter 6). As part of the retelling of the passion story we had discussed the relationship between Jesus being betrayed by a kiss, and how that particular form of betrayal might inform our own lives. Many people experience betrayal by their partners through illicit kisses with others and there was a relationship between that and this sculpture on the seafront. We chose a Des'ree song that had become famous as part of the soundtrack of the Baz Luhrmann film Romeo + Juliet and decided to overlay that with the account of Judas's betrayal of Jesus with a kiss.

Finally, we wanted the fifth location to close the trail in a positive way while still maintaining something of the sadness and austerity of Lent as people would be engaging with this throughout the season and we didn't want to pre-empt the resurrection hope of Easter. We decided on an image of crucifixion mixed with the hope of new life in the form of red roses, both an image of beauty in the flowers and pain in the thorns. I made a wooden cross that would fit in one of the windows of the Chapel Royal and one of our team wound it tightly with a white cloth and threaded deep red silk roses into the winding. Our card in the window quoted the story of the two thieves crucified alongside Jesus in Matthew 27 and the declaration by the centurion that 'surely he was the Son of God' (NIV).

We thought it would be good to have one main voice for all the audio and that this should be female, and my daughter Amy, who was following in my footsteps as a performer, took on the role of voiceover talent, apart from when the chief priests had to speak in one of the Bible passages, a role given to me. We recorded our scripts and our audio colleague set to work adding ambient audio to create an appropriate atmosphere for each piece.

Meanwhile I needed to work out how to place transmitters and mp3 players close to each location. The Brighthelm centre, tattoo parlour and Chapel Royal locations were easy as each building was able to provide us with a power socket which could be dedicated to us for six weeks and that was close enough to the art to work with the headphones. But the war memorial in the middle of Brighton and a sculpture on the seafront were going to be much more difficult. So I went out again scouting each location for a potential suitable building close by with people who might be sympathetic to our project.

The war memorial sits between two parallel roads that are about 50 metres apart and lined mostly with offices, so I started knocking on doors or going into reception areas with my strange request. On one of the roads was a bank which I had initially discounted as my experience of banks is that they are not easy places to deal with, even on banking enquiries, so I wasn't confident about an unusual request like this. I was pleasantly surprised to be given a meeting with the branch manager, who was very helpful and agreed straight away, as there was a power socket near one of their windows that looked out onto the memorial and it wasn't going to be any inconvenience to them to house this for us. I guess they saw it as part of their corporate social responsibility and we may well have featured in one of their internal reports about community engagement at some point.

Then on to the seafront sculpture, which was going to be a challenge as it stood on open ground on the promenade with no obvious easily accessible building nearby. I tried a few pubs across the road from the sculpture but it was clear very quickly that it wouldn't be wise to expect our highly portable and quite delicate kit to last for six weeks in a public space full of party people every night. I was beginning to feel that we might not pull this location off so I went down onto the beach to sit and think and pray. After a while I turned around to restart my search and found myself looking straight at a bar/restaurant that was directly under the sculpture at beach level. As it was mid-morning the place was only just opening up and the owner was busy cleaning and arranging furniture. He liked the idea and immediately took me through to the kitchen where there was an unused power point up on a shelf which we could have. I guessed it was pretty much right underneath the Kiss Wall and was perfect for us. Thank you, God!

Now the locations were all set, I wrote a letter to each of the venues letting them know exact dates when we would set everything up and who to contact if they had any issues. Finally, after

three or four weeks sorting out artworks, locations, content and logistics I set to with publicity in our usual style, producing an A5-sized promotional postcard with all the details of the event, a map to follow to find the five locations and details about a series of Sunday evenings when we would lead guided meditations during Lent. I produced a set of five placards to be placed at each location – a sign on a spike to be placed in the ground at the foot of the tree at station one, window placards at stations two and five and more signs for stations three and four which were to be taped to the pavement using duct tape left over from the Greenbelt Fingermaze you can read about in Chapter 4. The final act was to get the headphones installed ready for people to pick them up along with contact forms so we knew who had taken them.

Everything was set up, mp3 players were set to loop and connected to transmitters, publicity was distributed and we were all ready for Lent to begin. The conversations with shopkeepers, bank managers, restaurant owners and church leaders about getting this set up had already been hugely rewarding in terms of talking about the meaning of Lent and the reasons why I wanted to do this as part of my Christian commitment. What's more, the process of discussing what kind of content we thought would be appropriate and how we would create this had made us think really deeply about our own faith and engagement with these themes.

The most rewarding part of this venture was the three guided tours that I ran on Sunday evenings with groups of about a dozen turning up each time. I had deliberately timed the tours so that we always approached the beach at around sunset, which showed off the Kiss Wall in its absolutely best light. Walking towards this contemporary evocation of this simple physical act while listening to the emotional music build to a crescendo as we heard the words, 'Jesus said, "Judas, would you betray the Son of Man with a kiss?"', was profoundly moving.

Some who completed the journey said that they found encouraging new perspectives of a spiritual nature through seemingly mundane everyday features of Brighton. Others commented that the sense they felt when walking around town with headphones was as though they were starring in a special movie made just for them. Yet others merely appreciated the time taken out of busy everyday life to simply slow down, breathe, listen, reflect and enjoy doing something out of the ordinary.

A visitor to Brighton who came across the trail wrote this on our blog: 'Spent some time in the Lanes yesterday, and was chatting with my wife about, "Wouldn't this be a great place to be Church?" I guess you guys are it! What a great place to be walking the Way of Jesus.' This is such a lovely description of what we're attempting to do because Lent Through the Lanes was a way of pointing people to the presence of God right beside them. We found that using our ears we could open our eyes to the wonder of God present in the ordinary features of life all around us. Eugene Peterson's version of the Bible, called *The Message*, renders John 1.14 as: 'The Word became flesh and blood, and moved into the neighborhood.' It turns out cutting ourselves off from the bustle of life by wearing headphones (something so many do these days) can help us to focus on the divine in our midst.

Barbara Brown Taylor writes in *An Altar in the World*:

People encounter God under shady oak trees, on riverbanks, at the tops of mountains, and in long stretches of barren wilderness. God shows up in whirlwinds, starry skies, burning bushes, and perfect strangers. When people want to know more about God, the son of God tells them to pay attention to the lilies of the field and the birds of the air, to women kneading bread and workers lining up for their pay. Whoever wrote this stuff believed that people could learn as much about the ways of God from paying attention to the world as they could from paying attention to scripture.

For me this is just as true in an urban environment as it is when experiencing the wonders of nature, even though I know this is not true for everyone. I think it's just as possible to sense the divine in a pleasing piece of city-centre architecture as it is on a sun-soaked hill top. I can find God in the patterns of a town square pavement as much as I can in the rippling of the waves on the seashore. I just need to be receptive to that and for my heart and soul to be attuned to the way God can inhabit all of those things.

You will have locations near to you that could be used to direct the thoughts of passers-by towards God. There are the obvious ones such as church spires, churchyards or noticeboards. Almost every city, town or village will have a war memorial or something similar, which can be the locus for a reminder about mortality. There may be local natural landmarks that can help people to see the divine – a particularly majestic tree, a village pond, a view from a certain vantage point, a quiet nook overlooking a small stream. These could all be places for a relevant reminder of the creator of all, who is in all.

In more urban environments there are possibilities to place things that might remind others of God. These don't have to form part of a trail, they could be solo opportunities for epiphany which you can highlight with a well-placed notice, either permanent or temporary. Of course, if it is permanent you will need to get the permission of whoever has responsibility for that location, whether a private individual, business or local council. Keep an eye open for shop-window decorations that might fit some sort of Christian message and once you have an idea of what that might look like, approach the shopkeeper with a simple explanation of the idea and how it won't be any inconvenience to them and may even help their business. Watch out for graffiti that could be highlighted as relating to God: it's surprising how often religious themes crop up in street art.

If you're the kind of person who likes to listen to music while you walk or commute, try to be alert to the way that music might inform a spiritual approach to your environment. I don't mean that you should only listen to worship music or hymns as you travel around but try to use the imaginary world that music creates to enhance your vision of the world around you rather than close you off from it.

Remember that God is all around us – we just need to open our eyes and ears to understand.

Things to consider

- Think about ways to use technology innovatively, perhaps in ways it wasn't intended for.
- Make it easy for people to take part.
- Use the skills of your team to help enhance an event.
- Open your eyes to the possibilities of spiritual connections with already existent objects and locations.
- Be persistent in the implementation of your idea.

3

Interactive Installations

People of faith have been creating landmark objects and symbols about their faith since before the time of Jesus. The Hebrew scriptures are full of stories of altars being created on mountain tops and cairns of stones being left at places of significant religious experience. Since the time of Jesus, Christians have wanted to create landmarks to remind themselves and others about God and the incarnation, from simple roadside shrines, crosses mounted on hilltops and decorations about the life of Jesus in catacombs beneath our feet, through to stupendous cathedrals, monuments commemorating particular moments of revelation and tiny wall-mounted images of saints and martyrs dotted around many European cities. The many, many churches of various shapes and sizes located in every city, town and village across the country also serve as reminders of a Christian tradition and often provide a holy place of sanctuary for people who want to pray, reflect, meditate or simply sit to take a break from the stresses of daily life.

The possibilities for spiritual encounter inherent in found locations and pre-existent art is examined in Chapter 2 as part of an intentional spiritual trail but it is also possible to create fixed interactive installations that could create a holy moment for a casual passer-by. One such installation is the story of the Lent Cross.

Lent is a very fruitful time for creating art that has spiritual connotations for people. This has been true for hundreds of years and may be the reason for the development of phenomena such as the tradition of the stations of the cross. Having had some success with creating Lenten trails with the Easter Path and Lent Through the Lanes (Chapters 5 and 2), we thought we would try something static which would arrest the attention of people walking by rather than inviting interested parties to join an intentional trail. We wanted to catch people unawares and reach a wider public than those who might already be disposed to be a pilgrim.

The idea started from a realization that there still exists a vestigial folk memory about Lent and its relationship to abstention. Even if a person has no religious connection, they often have an understanding that Lent is about giving up something, usually chocolate. I came across this when speaking to a particular retailer about getting involved with the Easter Path. I approached a well-known artisan chocolatier in Brighton to see if I could get them involved. Their hilarious response was that they didn't really like to highlight Lent as it was not a great time for chocolate businesses as so many people gave it up, causing a detrimental effect on their sales! I usually do Lent assemblies in our local school and even children from families who have no religious affiliation know that Lent is a time to give something up.

So, starting from a point of wanting to find a way to ask people about what they could do without, we wanted to find a mechanism for them to interact with that would prompt them to think. We thought it would be a good idea to create little slips with a question on each side – 'What could you live without?' and 'What couldn't you live without?'. These would be in the form of a toy banknote, signifying that there was a cost to giving things up or staying with habits that might not be good for us.

The next question was what to do with these slips. The obvious answer was some sort of collection box and we chatted around what this box should look like, as we planned for it to be in place permanently for the six weeks of Lent. It had to be fairly substantial and ideally in a place where there would be a lot of pedestrian footfall. We could think of several locations for a cross-shaped box in the Brighton Lanes but before we approached the council, I knew we would need to have the design of the installation worked out so that they could be assured it was safe and not an obstruction.

At the time *The X Factor* was the biggest show on television and it amused us to design our cross with an oblique reference to this as it was the epitome of commercialism and so the antithesis of the values of Lent. So we decided the shape would be a straightforward X rather than the cruciform cross more usually associated with Christianity, and it would have the same feel as a donation box or feedback collection-point where you're invited to contribute your customer comments or thoughts. There is a small plastic and Perspex shop in West Hove and at various points in the life of Beyond I had occasion to ask for unusual items to be made there, and so I set about creating a diagram of what we wanted in order to get a quote for its construction.

The cross would be 1 metre high and 1.5 metres across with each arm of the cross being 30 centimetres wide. The whole thing would sit on a wooden base made of marine ply, which I would make, and the Perspex man said he could cut all the pieces to size, bevel the edges so that it fitted really tightly and drill construction holes for the bolts that he would also supply. We agreed a price and he gave me a 2–3-week time frame for delivery once I'd supplied him with the wooden foundation.

While this was being fabricated, I went out, armed with a tape measure, to scout a place in the Brighton Lanes where we could put this now that we knew what our installation was going to look like. I found a location at a junction in one of the pedestrianized parts of the Lanes that was perfect, as there was plenty of space right beside a handy tree which we could secure the cross to, so that it didn't wander around the Lanes courtesy of helpful late-night revellers. I then contacted Brighton and Hove City Council highways department to find out what we needed to do to get permission to put something in this location. To my surprise they were very relaxed about it and told me that as long as we understood we were responsible for it, that it wouldn't obstruct the highway and that we had public liability insurance, then they were happy for us to go ahead. This informal approach may not be the case with all councils so if you're planning on setting up something like this yourself it would be wise to check with your local authority first.

Having secured a location for the installation I needed to work out how we could encourage people to interact with it. I'd got very used to creating signage and fixing this to pavements with tape and there were also some posts and the tree at the location to which I could attach instructions. But we needed somewhere for people to pick up the Lent pledge slips and they'd need pens to fill these in. I went back to the site and approached the shops that surrounded it to explain what we were hoping to do and ask if they would hold batches of the slips for us. They were all amazingly accommodating and agreed to help us out; once again they could see that there was some benefit to them as it might increase footfall to their stores with the possibility of additional sales.

Three weeks later the cross was ready and so I went to pick it up; it was all in pieces ready to be constructed, like a piece of IKEA furniture but with fewer instructions. I was surprised at the number and variety of different constituent parts and only just fitted it all in my car. I was also caught out by the weight of 13 separate pieces of 12 millimetre-thick Perspex and realized what hard work it was going to be moving this around once the whole entity was constructed, especially with the wooden base. The Perspex guy had drilled bolt holes and cut corresponding threads with a tap and die set for a huge number of Allen key bolts to screw the whole object together. We figured that anyone who wanted to tamper with the cross once it was constructed was unlikely to be carrying an Allen key around with them so this ought to be secure.

The finishing touch to the design was to add the holes where we hoped people would post their pieces of paper. To prevent the possibility of rain going into the cross these were drilled slanting upwards so that there was no possibility of water running down the Perspex and getting the inside all wet. I also wanted to make sure people couldn't use the cross as an ash tray so the holes I drilled were slightly smaller than a cigarette, although of course this wouldn't prevent roll ups or lit matches being pushed through.

Ash Wednesday dawned, and a helper and I set off with all of the bits for the cross, a bag of tools, signage and stacks of the toy money slips. We spent a happy morning working out how to construct the whole thing, which was slightly more complicated than we'd thought, as the pieces had to be assembled in a certain order to make sure that the joins were water tight. I had attached a bracket to the wooden base and bought a cycle lock so that we could anchor the finished cross to the tree to prevent it being moved. We also used the tree as a base for some pens on strings and we stuck the signs to the pavement before giving the shopkeepers a pile of Lent pledge slips.

The notices made it clear that slips posted into the cross would eventually be used as part of an art exhibit at the Brighton Festival so that people adding their thoughts with this event were aware that whatever they wrote could be visible to others at a later date. They also featured information about Beyond including our website and phone number so people could get further information or call us if they had any concerns. We had decided to meet at the Lent Cross every Sunday in Lent at 3 p.m. for a short public act of sharing in bread and wine, and this was publicized on the notices along with a Holy Saturday event we planned for the end of Lent.

The final part of setting up was to roll up some of the Lent slips ourselves and post them into the cross as an example of what we hoped people might do. We got a good start for this as during the construction process people kept stopping to ask us what we were doing and once we'd explained it, asked if they could fill in a slip, so we already had a few genuine contributions from passers-by to start the interaction off.

I felt slightly sad and a little apprehensive as we walked away from our precious installation, leaving it all alone to the vagaries of public scrutiny, but we had done everything we could to make it safe and for it to be effective and thought-provoking. Something of the vulnerability of this artwork spoke to me of the openness of the incarnation. The way God entered the world as a defenceless baby, lived as a man with all the public scrutiny that Jesus was subjected to, and ultimately was exposed to danger and violence in the public square, which ended in crucifixion and death. Little did I know how much these themes would loom large over this project between its installation on Ash Wednesday and eventual finale on Easter day.

Four days later we were back at the cross for our first informal communion meal and I was gratified to see that new slips had been posted and that everything was pretty much exactly as we had left it on Ash Wednesday. One of the slips had unrolled itself as it lay on the floor inside the cross. On the 'What could you live without?' side the person had written 'My addiction'. I was moved by this personal confession from an anonymous contributor and this gave fuel to our prayers during our short act of worship. Using the cross as our table, paper plates and cups for the bread and wine, and simply using the words of institution from 1 Corinthians 11, half a dozen of us prayed and shared in food and drink as we stood at the cross. This simple act of devotion attracted a few people, who stopped and asked us what we were doing. We had Lent slips and pens with us and encouraged those who showed interest to contribute their own thoughts on what they could or couldn't live without. After an hour of public witness, we went on our way leaving the cross to its fate for the next seven days.

One of us checked on the cross every two or three days and were gratified to see more and more contributions gathering inside it. It was my turn to visit about three weeks after installation and I arrived to find it looking very different. It was still in place and functioning as we wanted it to, but someone had clearly tipped it up at some point and all the slips collected so far were piled in one arm of the cross. Large cracks had appeared at various places on the top and sides and on close inspection I could see footprints all over the top. It looked as though someone had been dancing on it (reminding me of that hymn 'Lord of the Dance') and the strain and weight of bodies and boots had cracked the cross in various places. The damage was mostly on the top but some of the sides also had stress fractures running from the bolt holes. Our decision to use thick Perspex and to bolt the whole thing together in multiple places had proved wise as the integrity of the container and presumably the safety of the dancers had been maintained.

So, what to do? I resolved to dismantle it, repair it as best I could and re-install it as quickly as possible. As it was still in one piece, I left it there for the next few hours while I went out and bought metal brackets and more bolts before going back, taking everything apart and transporting it home. Then followed a busy afternoon as I fitted metal braces across the cracks and added additional support to some of the bolts with large washers that helped to cover the smaller fissures. Finally, the pieces were repaired to my satisfaction and I took all of them back to the location and re-assembled the cross. Just to be on the safe side, I took about half the completed slips out and kept those at home in case there was more successful damage and someone managed to get in and take any slips.

I was quite pleased with the repaired cross with its shiny metal braces and patched-up scars. It had something of a Frankenstein

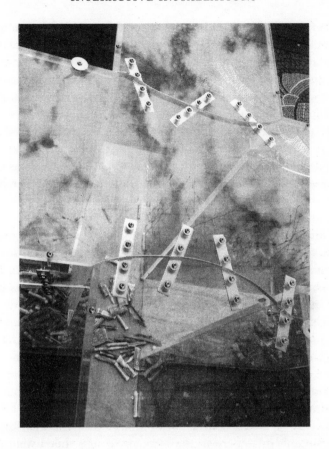

feel to it, but more importantly to me it bore the marks of the suffering it had been through during its sojourn in the city centre. There was something very powerful and redolent of the themes of Lent in the fact that this artwork had suffered and carried the scars of that suffering in the same way that Jesus carried the scars of his crucifixion even after his resurrection. Our communion celebration on the cross that following Sunday had added poignancy as the bread and wine rested on the cracks and metal brackets that now held the cross together.

Ten days later when doing my usual check, I discovered the cross plastered with flyers for a late-night club event entitled

'Worms'. This reminded me of the words that had begun Lent on Ash Wednesday at the imposition of ashes: 'Remember that you are but dust and to dust you will return. Turn away from sin and be faithful to Christ', although I don't imagine the club promoters were thinking of the decay of the grave when they titled their event. I didn't have to dismantle the cross to sort this out but got some solvent to soften the glue and removed the flyers without too much fuss.

Through all this the cross continued to fill with pledges so that now the floor of the installation was completely obscured by rolled up pieces of paper in a whole variety of different colours. Only ten more days until Easter.

Unusually for early April, Easter morning dawned beautifully sunny and crisp and I headed down to the cross early for the culmination of the Lent Cross experience after its six-week stay in this location. As I approached the Perspex box it glistened in the early-morning light, backlit by the low sun, casting translucent shadows on the ground, forming another cross-shape on the brick paving beneath it. It stood next to the bare branches of the birch tree that had been its anchor and companion throughout Lent, reminding me of the wood of the cross, hammered into service to carry the creator of the world on his final journey before death.

The whole area was strewn with rubbish from the night before and the only other person around that early on a Sunday morning was a lone street sweeper, carefully collecting up all the detritus of human life to take away in his cart; yet another metaphor for the work Jesus achieved through his crucifixion and resurrection. Alongside the piles of rubbish sat the heaps of pledges covering the floor of the cross, examples of the hopes and fears of a whole range of human debris that had flowed around this cross over the last six weeks. I took a moment before beginning the process of dismantling to consider all the humanity reflected in those little slips of paper and remembered the post-communion prayer we would be saying in church later that morning:

God of glory,
by the raising of your Son
you have broken the chains
of death and hell:
fill your Church with faith and hope;
for a new day has dawned
and the way to life stands open
in our Saviour Jesus Christ.
Amen.

I remembered that early slip that I had seen posted from the person wanting to be free of their addictions and prayed that this Easter all those who had felt the urge to contribute a thought on one of the slips would experience new hope, new life and freedom from whatever constrained them.

The installation endured bitter sea air and windy nights, people climbing all over it, beating it, kicking it, trying to unscrew it, promoting events on it, moving it, smashing it and sticking things to it. It collected copious amounts of bird droppings from the tree above but amazingly it was only smashed the once, meaning that it only had to be removed on one occasion for a little TLC, leaving it with scars that spoke powerfully of the treatment Christ received when he was beaten before eventually being nailed to a wooden cross. I felt a kinship with the women on that first Easter morning as I lovingly removed the screws that held everything together and collected up all the pieces and all the papers for a future resurrection as an art installation during the Brighton Festival a month later.

The exhibition took place in St Luke's Prestonville, the church where I am the parish priest, and for the first time brought together my life of art outside the church with my day job as a vicar inside the church. The Brighton Festival is one of the largest art festivals in Europe and we registered ourselves as part of the Festival Fringe under the title 'Home'. The exhibition would feature a number of different interactive exhibits that related to this general theme, the centrepiece being a huge map of Brighton and Hove that we had hand-painted onto a giant white tarpaulin. This took up all of the central floorspace of the church and visitors were invited to walk on the map and add to it any personal details relating to locations in the city using a marker pen.

Alongside this hung a wall made from the hundreds of Lent slips which had been posted in the cross during the previous month. Each of the 570 slips had been laminated, had holes punched in them, and then joined with treasury tags to make a wall 6 metres long, strung between two pillars in the church with one side showing all the contributions about 'things I could live without' and the other side being full of 'things I couldn't live without'. It was fascinating reading, ranging from the banal 'I couldn't live without my cat Jess' to the deeply profound 'I couldn't live without hope'.

It seemed that the side where people wrote about things they couldn't live without was much more profound than the other side. These included 'my individuality', 'the thought of tomorrow' and 'freedom'. It also included more mundane things like clothes, water, music as well as the occasional prayer – 'Please pray for my sister and family and keep them safe from harm'. Contributors did think deeply about the things they could live without and serious topics such as 'drama', 'worry' and 'child slavery' were mentioned among the trivial such as 'sweets' or 'chocolate'. Putting this together as a detailed artwork and chronicle of the 40 days of Lent was quite a moving process and the resulting artwork attracted a lot of attention as visitors spent time reading the comments.

One corner of the church had been turned into a totally white room with white walls, a white floor and simple white furniture. Visitors, and especially families, were invited to add coloured dots to any of the surfaces of the room, which was slowly being turned into an abstract work of art after an original idea by Yayoi Kusama, who was exhibiting at the Tate Modern at that time. The exhibition also included a large-scale artwork made using the surfboard masts that we still had from the original Blessing of the Surf installation (see Chapter 11). These were arranged into a tepee and the canopy of the tepee was fabricated from taped-together copies of the local free estate agent magazine. The exhibition was completed with a series of photographs mounted on hanging exhibition boards contributed by attendees to our monthly homeless drop-in.

These various artworks, apart from the floorcloth map, which only came out on Saturday and Sunday afternoons, remained in place throughout the month of May and our Sunday worship took place surrounded by this work, which served as a constant reminder during that month of the needs of those with no homes and how important home is for us all. It also informed the various weekday activities that took place in this church and it was interesting to see how attendees of various recovery groups, prayer meetings and the families who come to the parent/toddler group all interacted with the art in different ways.

The Lent Cross had a second life once again as an installation at the Greenbelt festival, mainly as an illustration of the damage and a visual representation of the pain of Lent. The wall of pledges was hung in one of the worship spaces at the festival and acted as a prayer wall for people between different scheduled acts of worship as well as being a screen behind which a number of large neon crosses had been installed, shining through the cracks in the wall and giving a holy glow to the different colours of the paper 'bricks' that formed this wall of human expression.

The mutilation that happened to the Lent Cross was part of a theme that occasionally reared its head in the work of Beyond, of artworks that were almost deliberately placed in order to decay or be damaged. We certainly became aware that placing art in a public space, especially for a period of time, opens it up to the possibility of vandalism, and this should always be considered when planning an exhibit of this type. Sometimes it cannot be predicted, as was the case with a car-sized ice sculpture which was intended to be a gentle reflection on the nature of time passing and the action of entropy on the whole of creation. What it turned into was a misshapen, discoloured lump of ice sat in a muddy puddle as people 'interacted' with it very heavily, including using keys or stones or lumps of concrete to scratch, knock or crack bits off the sculpture to try and get at the objects of beauty embedded within. This was upsetting for some, particularly those who had spent so much time working out how to achieve this artwork with a minimal budget and no experience, but to others it spoke powerfully of the way we treated Jesus on his journey to the cross.

The words of Isaiah 53 are often used in relation to this:

He had no beauty or majesty to attract us to him,
 nothing in his appearance that we should desire him.
He was despised and rejected by mankind,
 a man of suffering, and familiar with pain.
Like one from whom people hide their faces
 he was despised, and we held him in low esteem.
Surely he took up our pain
 and bore our suffering,

yet we considered him punished by God,
   stricken by him, and afflicted.
But he was pierced for our transgressions,
   he was crushed for our iniquities;
the punishment that brought us peace was on him,
   and by his wounds we are healed. Isaiah 53.2b–5 (NIV)

One of the things that artists long for is that their work provokes a response, and destruction of a work of art is a definite, if extreme, response. This fits with many Christian themes, especially around Lent and Easter but also in relation to sin and penitence, confession and absolution. There are also themes inherent in considering creation and our mismanagement of the planet that are all about destruction and decay. The heart of Christianity is a wonderful message of redemption and healing which brings hope to these difficult realities of life.

I believe our purpose as Christians creating art is also to hope to provoke a response which might open up the possibility of God for people. I think this is different from 'christian art', which is often all about conveying a specific message and can be seen as some form of evangelism. Art that creates opportunities for epiphany is missional in that it is seeking to express something of the *missio Dei* without seeking to explain it. Early on in the life of Beyond someone sent me an essay they had written from their experience of being involved in the Winchester Passion. This led them to conclude that there were three modes of evangelism:

Proclamation – this is the traditional understanding of evangelism, preaching on street corners, televangelism or mission events such as the Billy Graham crusades. This form of evangelism is not so well received in our postmodern world where people have a natural antipathy to being told what to do.

Pastoral – this is the Alpha-course approach to evangelism and involves small-group discussion, usually around a meal, so that people get to know each other and there are opportunities to share what Christian faith means to those who are hosting the group.

Parable – this is what events like the Winchester Passion do, simply tell stories and allow the audience to make their own mind up about what this means for them. This is the model mostly followed by Jesus, who used parables often and usually didn't bother to explain them. This is what I believe we're doing when we create art installations, especially when they're interactive. We're creating an artistic story about God which the participant can interpret in their own way with its own implications for them personally.

Beyond never intended to be a church. We were very clear from the start that we felt called to a particular role – creating arts events informed by our Christianity without any intention that participants would need to become members of anything. I felt very strongly that it was God's job to take people further if they wanted that. Beyond would offer to connect people to an appropriate local church if we were asked but the only ongoing contact we had was sometimes to ask people for email addresses so we could keep them informed of our events. We have high expectations of the way the Holy Spirit can work to transform the lives of those who interact with our work and don't want to put any institution or set of rules in the way to hinder that.

Things to consider

- Tap into cultural memory of faith themes.
- Make sure public artworks are well built and secured, especially in relation to the safety of all those who might engage with them.
- Get permission from relevant authorities for your installation.
- Provide self-explanatory signage for your artwork.
- Check the installation regularly.
- Be prepared for public art to be damaged.

4

Walking Meditation

One of the interesting trends of the last 20 years has been the rediscovery of the idea of pilgrimage as part of spiritual enlightenment. Popular pilgrim routes such as the Camino trail through Northern Spain to Santiago de Compostela are so busy with pilgrims these days that it's sometimes hard to find the peace and solitude that for many exemplify this form of spirituality. The opening up of newly discovered pilgrim trails such as the Old Way from Southampton to Canterbury in Southern England by organizations such as the British Pilgrimage Trust has added to this popular movement. But what if you don't have the time or stamina for such epic journeys but still want to experience some form of spiritual journeying? A labyrinth might be the answer for you.

Labyrinths come in all sorts of shapes and sizes and all sorts of locations, both permanent and temporary, but they all share a similar format. A labyrinth only has one path so you can't get lost, unlike a maze, which presents you with choices about your route, some of which lead to dead ends. When you enter a labyrinth you follow a circuitous route which eventually brings you to the centre, where you can pause before retracing your steps or simply leave. The format encourages the participant to see the path as a spiritual journey towards their inner self and allows opportunity for reflection, prayer and self-examination. A labyrinth walk is a pilgrimage of introspection inviting the pilgrim to spend time focusing on themselves and their relationship with God and to leave the distractions of the world at the beginning of the path for a few moments of 'me' time before returning to daily life.

Labyrinths can be found in all kinds of places, and some cathedrals have labyrinths laid out on their floors, the most famous one being in Chartres cathedral, which is over 800 years old. Labyrinths sometimes feature in monastery gardens or parks and on occasion creative folk have crafted temporary labyrinths by mowing a pattern in a grass lawn. There are mobile labyrinths which are painted on large canvas cloths that can be laid out on a church floor or in a community hall. I have friends who have made labyrinths on the beach at low tide with hundreds of pebbles which have then been washed away by the advancing sea.

In Hove we are lucky to have a unique permanent labyrinth in a local park, which was commissioned by the council from the artist Chris Drury. Originally it was a temporary structure cut into the grass of a different park, which proved so popular that the council asked the artist to create a permanent version as part of its Urban Cultural programme. It's called the Fingermaze because it is based on a giant fingerprint 50 metres long and 40 metres across and is ingeniously designed to incorporate all the whorls and lines of a normal thumbprint while 'hiding' a large-scale labyrinth within its coils. It can be viewed easily on the

satellite view of Google maps as it stands out beautifully against the green grass of Hove Park as a clear white image. We have used this installation for many years as a July event combined with a summer picnic, and each time have created a theme for the labyrinth walk. These themes can be easily translated to any other labyrinth of any size or type in another location.

The obvious theme to begin with was that of identity, since fingerprints are unique to each of us and can be used to identify us in all sorts of circumstances, especially if we've been involved in some nefarious activity. We decided to title our first use of this Godsend 'Who Am I?', creating a journey inwards to highlight different aspects of our identity and inviting the person journeying to consider these aspects and then leave each of them behind at a particular point in the labyrinth as though they were shedding this baggage along the way. They should then reach the centre of the labyrinth unencumbered just as themselves and be invited to contemplate who they really were before taking the journey back out and resuming en route the different roles that we all play in our daily lives.

We determined five themes to consider and so needed to set up five stations at various points along the route of the labyrinth. I spent some time pacing the whole Fingermaze and counting my steps so as to work out where to place each of these stations, and we bought five 2-metre-high galvanized garden spirals which could be stuck into the ground at the appropriate point on the walking route. We attached a couple of coloured helium-filled balloons to each stake to match five sets of different-coloured labels that I had created with different identity questions on them. These were:

- List the roles you play in life (mother, husband, daughter, manager etc.).
- How do you describe yourself to others?
- Where have you come from? What are the influences that formed you?
- What are your aspirations for yourself?
- How would you describe yourself spiritually?

Each person was given a set of pre-strung labels as they entered the labyrinth, and when they reached each station were invited to write an answer on the appropriate label and tie it to the stake before moving on. Once they had completed all five stations their journey would take them to the middle of the labyrinth, where there was a mirror and some verses from Genesis: 'God spoke: "Let us make human beings in our image, make them reflecting our nature ..." God created human beings; he created them god-like, reflecting God's nature. He created them male and female' (Genesis 1.26 and 27, *The Message*). This was accompanied by the message, 'You are unique', and an invitation to put a finger-print on the mirror using an ink stamp pad.

On the way back out of the labyrinth, the other side of the placards asking the identity questions featured different Bible verses about the same themes that the pilgrim had been encouraged to shed on their way in. All of these were taken from *The Message* version of the Bible as the language is so accessible and presented in a way that makes familiar verses of scripture come to life.

If you would like to use these verses for a meditation of your own, here they are:

SPIRITUALITY
God's Spirit touches our spirits and confirms who we really are. We know who he is, and we know who we are.
(Romans 8.16)

FUTURE
What a God we have! ... God is keeping careful watch over us and the future.
(1 Peter 1.3 and 5)

PAST
You formed me in my mother's womb.
I thank you, High God ...
Body and soul, I am marvelously made!
I worship in adoration – what a creation!
You know me inside and out,

you know every bone in my body;
You know exactly how I was made, bit by bit,
how I was sculpted from nothing into something.
Like an open book, you watched me grow from conception to
birth;
all the stages of my life were spread out before you,
The days of my life all prepared before I'd even lived one day.
(Psalm 139.13 and 14)

SELF
The God who made you in the first place says:
'Don't be afraid, I've redeemed you.
I've called your name. You're mine.
When you're in over your head,
I'll be there with you.
When you're in rough waters,
you will not go down.
When you're between a rock and a hard place,
it won't be a dead end –
Because I am God, your personal God.'
(Isaiah 43.1 and 2)

ROLES
So here's what I want you to do, God helping you:
Take your everyday, ordinary life; your sleeping, eating,
going-to-work, and walking-around life and place it before
God as an offering.
Embracing what God does for you is the best thing you can
do for him.
Don't become so well-adjusted to your culture that you fit
into it without even thinking. Instead, fix your attention on
God. You'll be changed from the inside out.
(Romans 12.1 and 2)

The day of the event dawned bright and warm and continued
into a beautiful sunlit evening, as two dozen people turned up
to join in with the Fingermaze event. We set up a gazebo as our

base for the picnic and had a wonderful time as people sat and chatted or took themselves off in their own time to walk the labyrinth. It was a great way to get to know each other better, to examine some of the themes that form us and our relationship with God and to relax in preparation for the summer holidays, but that wasn't the end of the Fingermaze for us that summer.

I had proposed that we attempt a recreation of this at the Greenbelt festival at the end of August. A central part of the site at Cheltenham racecourse was a broad expanse of tarmac between the grandstands and the horse parade ring. The organizers had given us the go-ahead to create a version of the Fingermaze on this concourse, subject to stringent health and safety concerns and with the proviso that we didn't damage or mark the tarmac. In preparation for this I had been testing out various types of white duct tape on the pavement outside my house to see which withstood the weather best and which didn't leave any mark once removed after a few days. My wife was slightly bemused by the half a dozen strips of white tape stretched across the ground just outside our gate, but I assured her it was necessary research for a very spiritual project!

Having selected a particular brand of tape and ordered a dozen rolls so that I was sure we had enough, I then set about the task of working out how we would translate the design to a location 130 miles away. I remembered a school lunchtime club from my childhood where we would make scale models of various airplanes using silhouettes from the *Observer's Book of Aircraft*, which we would scale up to the size we wanted by drawing a grid over the image and then transcribing this to a larger grid. The same technique could be used for the Fingermaze so I set about doing the maths to work out what size grid I would need and how to transfer this to a tarmac concourse.

I had a black and white image of the Fingermaze taken from a photo of the plaque about the artwork in Hove Park and after some complicated maths (at least complicated for me) I worked out that I could draw a small grid over this and transfer it to a larger grid of 1-metre squares once we got to Cheltenham. I made a 1-metre square wooden frame and we set off for the racecourse with my little drawing, my template square, a load of chalk and a kilometre of duct tape. Once there a team of volunteers set to on their knees to try and map this out.

I would lay down my frame and draw the labyrinth line for the particular square in chalk then flip the frame over to mark the next square of the grid and chalk that one in and so on. The willing helpers would then follow on using the chalk line as a guide for the duct tape and cleaning off the chalk as this was one of the forbidden materials.

It was back-breaking and knee-scouring work but after a whole afternoon of doing this we had a really good facsimile of the main portion of the Fingermaze which was 20 metres by 16 metres and covered an impressively large section of the concourse. I had prepared the placards about identity along with the Bible verses as signs which could be taped to the tarmac at the appropriate point in the labyrinth, and we had bought a set of stands to hold the garden stakes for people to attach their labels to. Every day we set up a little table with labels and instruction sheets, and a team member would sit and manage anyone who wanted to participate in the mini-pilgrimage. It was a quite different experience walking this labyrinth in the middle of a bustling busy concourse compared to the tranquillity of the park back in Hove but many people engaged with it and it created a very visible prayerful presence right at the heart of the festival.

This wasn't the end of this particular iteration of the Finger-maze identity meditation though. I was beginning to get asked to do talks about the work of Beyond and I found that people were really interested in the Fingermaze concept but wanted to know more and in particular were interested in how the detail of it worked. This was hard to explain in the middle of a talk and also I wanted people to experience this not just hear about it, so that set me off on a quest to produce a video.

Although I was working in television I was not a hands-on editor or animator, but through years of business presentations and talks I had become a dab hand at Keynote (the Mac version of PowerPoint) and with a bit of fiddling about I was able to create a video animation of the walk with an audio soundtrack. I have often used this eight-minute video meditation at the end of a talk about the work of Beyond and it's an ideal way to bring a moment of prayer and reflection to what otherwise would just be a lecture.

The idea of theming a labyrinth walk in some way became a regular opportunity for us to create something for this wonderful public space and so we returned every July for an early evening picnic and a chance to walk the Fingermaze, focusing on a differ-ent spiritual theme each year.

One of these was the (Me)ditation, which followed similar themes to the original 'Who Am I?' event. In this case participants found a big pile of pebbles at the entrance to the Fingermaze and they were loaded up with ten of them to carry with them on their journey around the labyrinthine path. As they juggled with the challenge of not dropping anything they were reminded of all the different factors we juggle in our lives and the burdens we often carry around with us every day. Once again stations came into play as part of the journey and these highlighted different aspects of our lives that can prove difficult, such as work, rela-tionships, family, health or the environment. The thoughts about these themes were presented on black cards as a reflection of the difficulties that we often experience, and there was an invitation to let go of a pebble at each station and leave it there as a way of releasing themselves from the burden of that.

Ten stations later the walker would reach the centre of the labyrinth unencumbered by all their cares and not having to carry anything. The placard there then asked them to turn around and retrace their steps; here they would come across the same themes but now in a positive light on white card, and be given an opportunity to pick up a flower as a sign that this part of their lives could be about fulfilment, not a burden. By the end of their labyrinth walk each participant would have replaced all their burdensome pebbles with a beautiful bunch of flowers.

One obvious approach for this installation was to pick up on the original labyrinth story from Greek mythology of Theseus, Ariadne and the Minotaur. The story goes that Theseus was due to be sent into the labyrinth to be devoured by the half-man, half-bull monster Minotaur, but Ariadne, who had fallen in love with him, gave him a golden thread so that he could find his way out of the labyrinth after slaying the monster with a concealed sword. If you remember the beginning of this chapter you may be aware of a flaw in this story, which seems to have confused a labyrinth with a maze because a labyrinth only has one route and so there's no need for any form of guidance to help you get in or out. But that doesn't lessen the impact of the story or our hope to use it for spiritual purposes.

We thought that we would reference this myth by giving everyone who entered the labyrinth a ball of wool and ask them to pay this out behind them as they made their journey through the twists and turns of the walk. To add some spiritual input to the walk we gave everyone an mp3 player with an audio meditation and some verses of scripture as a way of shaping their thinking as they walked. In the centre of the Fingermaze we installed a small dead tree that would come into play later on during the event.

I wrote a script for the audio meditation and had some friends record this with a child reading 'the voice of God' excerpts from the Bible, helping to guide our thoughts as the labyrinth was traversed. This is the script; once again all the Bible quotes are from *The Message*:

Step into the Fingermaze.

Lay the thread behind you as you walk.

Enjoy the music and the chance to be alone with your thoughts and with God.

Listen to God's words:

> Be careful to do what God has asked of you; do not turn aside to the right or to the left. Walk in the way He has commanded you, so that you may live and prosper and prolong your days in the land that he has promised you.

Notice the feel of the ground as you walk.

> Observe the commands of God, walking in his ways and revering him. For He is bringing you into a good land – a land with streams and pools of water, with springs flowing in the valleys and hills.

Notice whether you're walking up the slope or down.

> Even though I walk through the valley of the shadow of death, I will fear no evil, for you are with me; your rod and your staff, they comfort me.

> The people walking in darkness have seen a great light. On those living in the land of the shadow of death a light has dawned.

Look at how the light falls around you as you move.

> Blessed are those who have learned to acclaim God, who walk in the light of God's presence.

> God's word is a lamp to my feet and a light for my path.

Consider how far you have come on this journey.

Wonder at how far you still have to go.

> God's love is ever before me, and I walk continually in His truth.

Teach me your way, O God, and I will walk in your truth;
give me an undivided heart, that I may fear your name.

Be aware of your physical condition as you walk.

Those who hope in God will renew their strength. They will
soar on wings like eagles; they will run and not grow weary,
they will walk and not be faint.

What does God require of you? To act justly, to love mercy
and to walk humbly with Him.

Blessed are those who do not walk in the counsel of the wick-
ed or behave like sinners or sit in the seat of mockers.

How do you relate to others?

And this is love: that we walk in obedience to God's com-
mands. As you have heard from the beginning, his command
is that you walk in love.

Are others walking around you?

God says I will walk among you and be your God, and you
will be my people.

If we walk in the light, as God is in the light, we have fellow-
ship with one another.

Walk humbly with your God until you reach the end of your
journey at the centre of the Fingermaze.

The day came for the event and it turned out to be cold and
grey with quite a strong breeze which put a bit of a dampener
on the picnic, but still a number of people turned up to explore
the labyrinth and see what spin we had put on it this year. As
they started their walk it became clear that laying a flimsy piece
of wool behind you with the wind blowing was not so easy, so
some of our volunteers stepped in as 'woolwalkers' who followed behind the participants helping to lay their wool trail on
the ground and keeping it there. Even so the wool blew around,

leaving the confines of the path and spreading across the grass, forming a spiderweb pattern across the whole Fingermaze.

There were many things to learn from the walking – how difficult it was to keep the thread running between the lines of the Fingermaze, how some people outstripped their woolwalker with the speed of their walking, what people did when the wool ran out before they reached the centre of the maze (some stopped, others continued, some fetched additional wool to complete the trail). All of us learnt a lot about ourselves as we focused inwardly through listening to the meditation and walking.

Once everyone had completed their walk, the Fingermaze was transformed by the coloured trails that now draped their way around the labyrinth, adding a track of bright colour to the green grass in the gloomy evening light. At this point I asked everyone to gather around the edge of the Fingermaze for one last ritual act. Once we had a complete circle of people, I invited everyone to move towards the middle gathering up the wool as they walked so that the park wouldn't be littered with wool.

Once we reached the middle we draped the wool, which was mostly shades of orange and red, onto the dead tree, turning it from a dull brown lifeless object into a beautiful burning bush that formed the centre of an afternoon traversing holy ground. Though we walk through this life on a single path, it criss-crosses the paths of others and joins with them in community. It's in these communities that we often experience God's holy ground which underpins us all and is the foundation of the world.

Afterwards I had a deep conversation with one of the participants, who told me of their frustration with the wool as they walked the labyrinth. They wished they could stop looking back to see if the wool was going in the right place and how they wanted just to listen to the meditation and the relief they felt when their ball of wool ran out and they could stop looking back and focus on what lay ahead. They realized that this represented their life, which had been pretty difficult over the past few years, but that they just needed to stop looking back and let God lead them into a new future. This was God working in that person's life to bring an epiphany. Our goal is always to try to create opportunities for epiphany, environments where God can show up and change people or bring some kind of revelation that can transform their life.

We used mp3 players again on the final Sunday in a series of events on Fire, Earth, Water and Air. We all know that air is essential to life and the evening offered an opportunity to explore this miracle that governs every minute of our lives and to see it as an example of God's presence and life. In the Hebrew scriptures the word *Ruach* is often translated as 'spirit', which is its primary sense, but it also means 'breath', 'air' or 'wind'. Similarly in the New Testament the Greek word *pneuma* has usually been rendered as 'spirit' but could equally be translated as 'breath' or 'wind'. So the phrase 'Spirit of God' could just as easily be written 'Breath of God' or 'Wind of God' in our Bibles. This makes a connection to the divine with every breath that we take, and this felt like a good theme to reflect on as part of our labyrinth walk.

When we arrived in the park, on what turned out to be another beautiful sun-kissed July evening, we found a large family group having a picnic quite close to the Fingermaze. They had been there all afternoon celebrating the birth of a baby and conducting an informal baby-naming ceremony. I explained what we were planning to do and we had an interesting discussion about names, christening and baptism in relation to their celebration. I invited them to join in once we'd set everything up and introduced them to the ideas that we were focusing on that evening.

The Fingermaze was decked out with some mirrors and a large balloon in the centre. We had stacks of little flasks of bubble liquid and some of the volunteers took turns to blow bubbles across the sunlit labyrinth: we had positioned ourselves upwind of the installation so all our bubble-making flowed across the grass where people were walking. Each of the mirror stations contained a placard with a Bible verse and the invitation to breathe on the mirror so that it steamed up and would reveal a simple image that had been traced on the glass with a wet finger. It was quite amusing to see some of the folk from the baby-naming group christen the installation by walking the labyrinth and reading the Bible verses to each other in their gently inebriated state. There was a lot of alcohol-infused heavy breathing going on as they tried to get the images on the mirrors to reveal themselves!

When a walker reached the middle of the labyrinth, they found a large helium-filled balloon attached to a basket full of little phials of bubble liquid on which the word *Ruach* had been written. The instructions told them that the bubble mixture was for them to take away as a reminder of the breath and spirit of God. As the basket slowly emptied, the weight holding the balloon down was lessened until it was straining at the tether that was holding it to the ground, a visible sign of the spirit at work.

On another occasion we used water in preparation for an installation we planned to set up at Greenbelt called 'Inner Refreshment'. At the entrance to the Fingermaze was a pile of paper cups and a large bucket full of dirty water. Participants were asked to fill a cup to the brim with the water and to make their journey through the labyrinth, spilling as little of the water as possible, which was quite tricky on the uneven ground, and using this as an opportunity to think about things they would like to cleanse from their life. To give this some context there was a verse from Ezekiel 24.13 to set them thinking: 'You mix uncleanness with obscene conduct. I tried to cleanse you, but you are not clean' (NET).

On reaching the centre of the labyrinth they found a cross and attached to it was a device called a Lifestraw. This is a filter that can be used to create safe, clean drinking water in any situation; it's utilized especially in places in West Africa where clean water isn't always easily obtainable. Each person could pour their dirty water into the filter, which would drain into a large bucket with a tap dispensing clean water for the journey out of the labyrinth. This was accompanied with a quote from Jesus: 'If anyone is thirsty, let them come to me and drink' (John 7.38, NET).

In our years at the Hove Fingermaze, we've also had nature-themed meditations; invited people to focus on their senses of touch, taste, smell, sight and sound; we've timed the event to happen at sunset so that we could allude to themes of dark and light; planned one on harmony using different sources of musical notes spread around the labyrinth but unfortunately had to cancel that due to bad weather. We even managed to find some ways to reflect spiritually on themes of independence and isolation by focusing on the story of the road to Emmaus following the UK referendum result to leave Europe.

There are endless ways to theme a meditative walk to provide some sort of spiritual focus for the participants. You can add these to a labyrinth near you or create a labyrinth of your own, and there are plenty of designs and sets of instructions about how to do this on the internet. You may choose just to invite people to join you on an intentional spiritual walk and have some thought prepared for people to focus on as you walk. The important thing is to have a broad topic without necessarily expecting an outcome. Use Bible verses related to your chosen theme to help stimulate the conversation or the thought processes in an open way, allowing God to speak to the participants in a way that is appropriate to them.

We often use a blessing to go with our walking meditation that is adapted from words by John O'Donohue called 'May The Light Of Your Soul Guide You':

May God guide you.
May God bless your walk with the secret love and warmth of your heart.
May you see in your walk the beauty of your own soul.
May the sacredness of your walk bring healing light and renewal to you and to those who walk with you.
May your walk never weary you.
May it release in you wellsprings of refreshment, inspiration and excitement.
May you be present in what you do.
May you never become lost in bland absences.
May the walking never burden you.
May your beginning find you awake and alert, approaching your walk with dreams, possibilities and promises.
May you find grace and fulfilment as you walk.
May you finish blessed, sheltered and protected.
May God calm, console and renew you.

Things to consider

- A walking meditation could just follow a natural feature such as a nature trail or coastal walk; the key is to add spiritual intention to the walk.
- Is there a labyrinth near you that could be used?
- Can you create a labyrinth using tape on tarmac, a design mown into a lawn, pebbles marking out the design or some other material (rope, chalk, paint?).
- Create a theme for your spiritual walk and consider how to create places to pause and reflect along the trail.
- Does the location or design of your trail suggest any appropriate themes for the walk?

5

Retail Spirituality

I am the opposite of a shopaholic. I am not a devotee of the cult of retail therapy, unlike so many people today for whom shopping is not just a necessity but a leisure activity in itself, a sport to be engaged in on a regular basis to help pass the time and as a shared activity with friends. Indeed, shopping is for some a ritual activity, indulged in with religious intensity akin to the devotion given in former years to worship. The days when Sunday was a sacred day of rest on which most shops were closed and there was nothing much else to do except go to church are long gone, and shopping malls are the modern cathedrals of consumerism, swarming on Sundays with devotees who have gone to worship the god of retail.

So how can we engage with this demographic who are using their leisure time in this way, who often head to the shopping mall because they don't have anything else to do and who might be open to being distracted as they window-shop and are looking for something to engage their interest? I believe window-shopping and even grocery shopping are potential avenues of spiritual exploration and are ripe opportunities for public engagement in matters of faith.

The Lanes in Brighton are a shopping mecca full of small, independent, unusual and quirky shops selling everything from vegan shoes to high-end designer suits, and this became the setting for an artistic/retail version of stations of the cross.

The concept was simple – persuade a dozen or so shop owners in the Lanes to give over a small portion of their shop window to an artwork loosely based on one of the stations of the cross. Each window installation would have a placard with some thoughts for reflection and instructions about where to find the next artwork so this would form a trail around the streets of Brighton that intentional pilgrims could take or which, more importantly, could ambush casual shoppers into a spiritual experience.

I thought I'd try the idea by approaching the owners of a cycle shop who I vaguely knew through church connections. I explained the concept to them but they didn't think this would be possible for them as the chain-link security shutter on their window was broken and permanently stuck across the window. Thinking on my feet, I pointed out that this fixed metal grid reminded me of a prison and that I thought this could be made into the station where Jesus was bound and imprisoned. This opened their eyes to the possibility that this might work and so they agreed to take part, subject to seeing the artwork we proposed. So I knew that at least one shop owner was on board and that the project had potential and was beginning to be a possibility. I set out to find other shops willing to take part now that the cycle shop was already in the bag.

The trail needed to make geographical as well as theological sense, and so I wanted station one to be fairly close to the cycle shop and for each subsequent station to be a short walk further on, taking any participants on a journey, but not expecting them to hike for miles between artworks. There was a United Reformed Church and community centre quite nearby and I knew that the minister there had creative aspirations, so I asked him if he would like to be involved. He agreed and so his church café window became station one with a specifically created piece of collage art about the garden of Gethsemane looking out onto one of the main thoroughfares in the centre of the city.

It was just a five-minute walk to the cycle shop, which became station two of this art trail. So as to follow the Easter story this had to continue the narrative after Jesus' betrayal in the garden and this is where the malfunctioning security grille came into play. One of our team bought a wax moulding kit and her husband was the model as she used him to fashion two beautiful life-size wax hands which we roped together with some old-fashioned

hessian rope and affixed to the prison-like security grille. This became 'Jesus was arrested'.

In one corner of the window we fixed an A4 placard explaining about the trail with these words:

> The Easter Path is a BEYOND initiative and features 12 Easter themed art installations or stations in shop windows in central Brighton.
>
> For more information you can pick up a leaflet inside or go to www.beyondchurch.co.uk.

This appeared in every window that was part of the trail and alongside this was a text box giving directions to the next station.

Every window also had a short Bible passage and some words to reflect on, which were customized for each location. The cycle shop window placard was labelled as station two and the text said:

Jesus is condemned
Jesus was taken to the Roman governor, Pilate, to be judged and sentenced.

The image of God being bound and restrained by human hands is extremely powerful and reminds us of the incredible power that we have and how cruel people can be. The ropes holding him are a reminder of what is to come as Jesus is flogged and humiliated before being taken to the cross to die

followed by some words from Mark 15:

They bound Jesus, led him away and handed him over to Pilate … 'What shall I do, then, with the one you call the king of the Jews?' Pilate asked them. 'Crucify him!' they shouted. 'Why? What crime has he committed?' asked Pilate. But they shouted all the louder, 'Crucify him!' Wanting to satisfy the crowd, Pilate released Barabbas to them. He had Jesus flogged, and handed him over to be crucified. Mark 15.1b, 12–15 (NIV)

A comic shop was the location for station three and illustrated how the process of creating the trail became an interesting opportunity to have conversations about spirituality with shop staff as well. The assistants in the store were interesting to talk to, but their initial reaction was to decline the offer to be involved because they didn't think religion had anything to do with them and their world. But I got a call from them a few weeks later to say they had reconsidered because so many of the comics and graphic novels that they loved were about gods and heaven, death and resurrection, and they were happy to take part as long as they could control their own window display. I was delighted that they had engaged with this subject so deeply and been talking about it among themselves. I was also pleased that we wouldn't have to dream up an artwork for their window and I left it up to them to create whatever they felt was most appropriate.

One of the principles that I always try to put into practice when collaborating with people who have no church background is to let them interpret the theme in the way that they want. This is not only respectful of their opinions but also opens my mind to possibilities and alternatives that are not part of my faith experience. This is obviously a bit risky as the end result could well be outside the realms of Christian orthodoxy, but as long as it's not offensive and is the authentic opinion of those who create it then I think that's OK. It also gives us a window into the minds of those outside of religion and helps us to see our world from their perspective.

In this case the shop produced a simple cross-shaped display in the window using cover images from an edition of a comic called Final Crisis. This series brings together a number of super-heroes and in each edition one of them is killed by 'Darkseid', a force colloquially known as 'the god-killer'. This demonstrated a depth of understanding of the themes of Lent and Easter that astonished me. I could never have come up with something more appropriate for a Lent journey towards the cross which was relevant to the clientele that would use this shop and who would understand the subtleties of this message!

The placard that accompanied this said:

Jesus receives the cross

Jesus is made to carry the instrument of torture that will eventually be used to kill him. Comics and graphic novels are full of stories of superheroes who die and are resurrected. The Final Crisis series featured in this cross design has major characters such as Batman being destroyed by what Superman describes as a 'god-killer' and a crowd of heroes attending a funeral at which they pray for resurrection.

Station four was a picture-framing shop that allowed us to put whatever artwork we liked into one of their frames; they even donated the frame! This became one of the stations where Jesus falls. If you know the traditional stations of the cross, you will know that Jesus falls three times, and this was a simple line drawing illustrating someone falling over, with little arrows like some kind of scientific diagram. The text that accompanied this referred to our own human frailty:

Jesus falls

The story tells us that Jesus fell a number of times while carrying his cross. This shows us that he suffered weakness and fatigue in the same way that we do. Jesus was far from being a super-hero God who uses extraordinary powers to overcome all, but was someone who shared our human frailty and understands how hard life sometimes gets.

And a Bible passage from Galatians reinforced this, as we didn't always want the scripture references to be confined to the Easter story:

I suspect you would never intend this, but this is what happens. When you attempt to live by your own religious plans and projects, you are cut off from Christ, you fall out of grace. Meanwhile we expectantly wait for a satisfying relationship with the Spirit. For in Christ, neither our most conscientious religion nor disregard of religion amounts to anything. What matters is something far more interior: faith expressed in love. Galatians 5.4–6 (*The Message*)

Station five was a multifaith 'spirituality store' that sold everything from crucifixes to buddhas, tarot cards to rosary beads. They gave us a statue of Mary, which we used as the station where Jesus meets his mother.

Jesus meets his mother

This is one of the most poignant moments in the Easter story as mother meets son in the worst circumstances possible. Seeing anyone who has been beaten and humiliated is a terrible experience, but this is even worse for those who are linked by blood and shared history. Imagine what it must feel like to see someone you love in a situation such as this.

Station six was the office window of the firm of accountants who looked after my finances. They shared the building with an estate agent and so we created a cross-shaped collage of images in collaboration with a local charity that helps homeless folk, and this became the station when Simon of Cyrene steps in to help Jesus carry his cross, mirroring all those charities which step in to help those in need.

Jesus is helped by Simon of Cyrene
While Jesus struggles with his cross he is aided by one of the bystanders in the crowd. This collage of images of people helping and being helped has been put together by Off The Fence, a Brighton & Hove charity which provides help for the homeless, women at risk and vulnerable young people in our city.

Once again the scripture accompanying this came from somewhere other than the Easter story:

'"I was hungry and you fed me, I was thirsty and you gave me a drink, I was homeless and you gave me a room, I was shivering and you gave me clothes, I was sick and you stopped to visit, I was in prison and you came to me." Then they are going to say, "Master, what are you talking about? When did we ever do any of these things for you?" Then God will say, "I'm telling the solemn truth: Whenever you did one of these things to someone overlooked or ignored, that was me – you did it to me."' Matthew 25.35–40 (*The Message*)

Station seven was a Christian bookshop in the heart of town. They gave us a nice big space in their window to hang a cloth with a graffiti image of the face of Jesus sprayed onto it. We took the image from some graffiti that had appeared on a rusty pillar remaining from the ruin of the West Pier on Hove seafront, giving this a real local connection. We also used this as the hero image to promote the event and which appeared on every placard as a way of identifying all the windows with each other. This stop on the trail told the story of Veronica, who stepped forward to wipe Jesus' face, starting a tradition of cloths purporting to hold an image of Christ as his sweat was imprinted onto the cloth.

Veronica wipes Jesus' face

This part of the Easter story gives us a tantalizing glimpse into the identity of Jesus as it gives rise to a number of images of Jesus' face imprinted into Veronica's cloth by his sweat and blood. The image on this cloth is reproduced from a piece of graffiti which has been placed on the West Pier by a mystery artist who has used the pre-existent barbed wire halo as a perfect image of Jesus wearing the crown of thorns.

Station eight was another city-centre church who gave over a window to a proper piece of art created by a local artist who drew a sensitive charcoal sketch of Jesus contemplating his own fall. It showed a person deep in thought, a glimpse into the mind of Christ as he falls once again.

Jesus falls

As Jesus makes his way through the streets to his execution place, he falls again.

This artwork challenges us to consider Jesus' frame of mind as he experiences more weakness and frailty. Jesus the man shares in the feelings of failure and despair that we sometimes experience, especially when times are difficult. He knows what it feels like to lose confidence in ourselves and to feel as though we are failing.

Followed by a short passage from Hebrews:

We have a great high priest, who has gone into heaven, and he is Jesus the Son of God. That is why we must hold on to what we have said about him. Jesus understands every weakness of ours, because he was tempted in every way that we are. But he did not sin! So whenever we are in need, we should come bravely before the throne of our merciful God. There we will be treated with undeserved kindness, and we will find help. Hebrews 4.14–16 (CEV)

Station nine was a newsagent window featuring the women of Jerusalem weeping – more of that later.

Station ten proved to be quite controversial. Initially I had a warm reception from the owner of a bespoke men's outfitters who not only agreed to take part but gave me a suit jacket to slash open and display on a cross-shaped stand in the window. I placed it in the window with the slashed back facing the street and attached some bright red silk behind the gashes in the jacket to represent blood. This looked great and was installed on Ash Wednesday, but by the following weekend it had disappeared. A chat with the shop owner revealed the fact, previously unknown to me, that he was Jewish, and his wife, who was more engaged with her faith than he was, had taken real umbrage at the installation and had taken it down.

After some considerable discussion with both of them it was agreed that it was acceptable to turn the jacket around so the slashes weren't visible and add a discreet lapel badge on it made from a pair of dice, representing the soldiers casting lots for the robe of Jesus. I gave the shop owners a range of different window placard texts and allowed them to choose the one they were most comfortable with, as understandably they weren't happy about having Christian scripture in their window; so we ended up with:

The soldiers throw lots for Jesus' robe
The robe that Jesus wore was unusual in that it was woven as a single item and so the soldiers threw dice to decide who should have it rather than divide it up. We often use clothes as a way of defining who we are and making a statement about ourselves. Fine clothes help us to feel good about ourselves and convey a message to those around us about our status and place in society.

After this adjustment both the owner and his wife were happy to let this stay there for the duration of Lent, which was just as well because I had already printed 5,000 flyers outlining the whole path, including this location. It was good to resolve this issue, not only because it was important to me that every retailer hosting our art was happy but because it also became an example of positive interfaith dialogue.

Most of the time we created bespoke work to fit the shop, but sometimes I would find shops that already had something that we could incorporate into the trail, like the architectural salvage shop that already had a five-foot-high wrought iron cross from France in their window. This became station 11 and the climax of the story when Jesus dies:

Jesus dies on the cross
This is the darkest moment in the Easter story and the climax of everything that has gone before. There are times when we all feel abandoned by God and that the world is a lonely, desolate place. Death will come to us all and the crucifixion reminds us of our own mortality and eventual destiny with stark reality.

Unfortunately, we almost had to abandon this station halfway through Lent as a shop assistant sold the crucifix not realizing it was part of our trail! I got a panicked call from the owner when he found out and we had to source an emergency cross to replace it until Easter.

Station twelve completed the trail and also featured art that was already in place in the seafront workshop of a neon artist who was repurposing bits of old fairground rides and had happened to create a couple of five-foot-high neon crosses. We were able to reference his work in the placard with an accompanying Bible quote:

Jesus is removed from the cross
The principal symbol of Christianity is an empty cross which no longer carries the image of the crucified Christ. This reminds us that after the crucifixion there was resurrection and that we follow a God who is alive and works in our lives through the power of the Holy Spirit. These crosses are made from pieces of old fairground lights that have been given a new life in this wonderful art form.

What a God we have! And how fortunate we are to have him, this Father of our Lord Jesus! Because Jesus was raised from the dead, we've been given a brand-new life and have everything to live for, including a future in heaven – and the future starts now! 1 Peter 1.3–4 (*The Message*)

This particular station began a number of collaborations with this artist, who also realized that there was a commercial opportunity here and started to produce smaller, domestic-sized crosses for home use which proved to be surprisingly popular.

In total the trail encompassed 12 locations within the centre of the city, creating an Easter Path that took about an hour to complete overall and involved a walk of almost two miles. The trail was in place for the whole six weeks of Lent, 24 hours a day, and it's impossible to know how many casual shoppers engaged with it over that time, but the potential footfall past these installations would have been many thousands. Some groups made special trips to Brighton to experience the trail and we ran guided tours at various points during Lent, culminating in a Good Friday pilgrimage as an alternative to the traditional Good Friday walks of witness that often take place in some towns.

One of the important aspects of an art trail of this nature is the unexpected associations that occur when you place something spiritual into a real-world, everyday environment.

As mentioned earlier, one of the installations was in a news-agent window in the centre of the Brighton Lanes. The shop owner was only able to give us a small window pane in one corner of his shopfront and the story we needed to tell was Jesus meeting the women of Jerusalem. Headline news at the time was an escalation of violence between Israel and Palestine (as is sadly so often the case) and the newspapers were full of images of Palestinian mothers mourning the loss of their sons in conflict. We took some of these images and photocopied them onto acetate and pasted these onto the glass of the window and positioned a light behind them to highlight this.

Our intention was simply to make an association between the women weeping in Gaza in current times and the women weep-ing at the treatment of Jesus 2,000 years ago. When we got to this station during the guided trail on Good Friday, one of the participants stood staring at the window for some time, deep in thought. After a few moments he began to move away and I asked him what he was thinking as we continued our walk. He told me he felt that the weeping women were all looking at the rest of the newsagent's window, which was full of glamour magazines and glossy images of supermodels. He was struck by the contrast between the pain and sorrow of so many women and the pressure we put on them to gloss this over and present a superficial face to the world. He commented that for him the pain of Good Friday and Jesus' journey to the cross was a reminder of the realities of life for so many versus the false images we are so often presented with through the media.

This is another example of an unexpected epiphany, a reve-lation from God that brings some spiritual enlightenment to someone. Ultimately as Christians who want to engage with mission, we want to create spiritual events that provide opportun-ities for God to be revealed. That revelation may not be the one

that we had intended, that is up to God. All we should be seeking
to do is to create an environment where God can work. That
applies just as much to the creation of a Sunday worship service
as it does to a faith-inspired art installation, a prayer meeting or
a spiritual event.

Retail spirituality doesn't have to be limited to staying on
the street and just window-shopping; with a bit of courage and
diplomacy it's possible to do something inside a shop as well.
The Supermarket Harvest is an example of that.

Most people have access to a supermarket and probably visit
their preferred store pretty regularly, surrounded by promotional
items, advertising signage and special offers. But what if some of
that marketing space could be turned to spiritual use? Thinking
along these lines led to the Supermarket Harvest, where the visit
to do a weekly grocery shop could also become an opportunity
to nudge people to think about God.

The idea was to use different sections of the supermarket to
prompt shoppers to pause for a moment, lift their eyes from
their grocery list and consider more eternal things. As a shopper
perused the bread aisle they would come across a small notice
with some words about Jesus as the bread of life and a prompt
to think about those who don't have enough to eat. Approaching
the wine department, a sign would remind them of Jesus' words
at the last supper to drink this in remembrance of him and that
he died that our sins might be forgiven. This journey continues
past the shelves of water and Jesus' promise to give the water of
life to those who ask, before we move on to the olive oil, where
words from Psalm 23 tell us that God anoints us with goodness
and mercy. Hardly any section of the supermarket is left out as
the sight and smell of fruit prompts us to think about the fruit
we produce in our own lives, and the meat and fish remind us to
thank God for the creation of the whole world and everything
in it.

The placards that were created for this were very simply
designed, with hardly any words, so that they were easy and
quick to read and kept to a minimum size so as not to take up
too much shelf space. I did not realize this but supermarket

suppliers have arrangements for the amount of shelf space that their product is displayed on and sometimes pay for promotional labels and signage to help support their particular products, so it's important not to impinge on those commercial deals. Sometimes it's better to put the Harvest signage on pillars or even in an A frame so that they are not taking up any shelf space at all, as long as this isn't getting in the way of shoppers.

As an addition to the signage, or even as an alternative if the store manager is not happy about displaying these messages, we produced a leaflet about the project that included the trail and all the same information that was presented on the shelves. These were handed out at the door, giving us an opportunity to talk to people as they entered to explain what we were doing and why. It was particularly good to talk to families with children and to encourage the children to take part by seeing if they could find the posters and match them to the sections on the flyer as they went round.

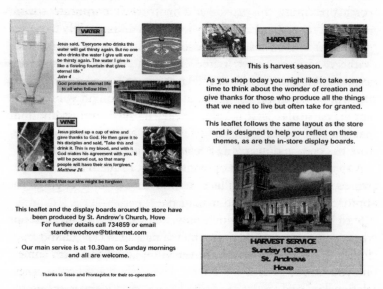

It would be possible to turn this into a treasure hunt and set the children the task of finding a particular quote or clue from every section and ticking it off on their sheet in return for a prize if they find the whole set. That would also give us a chance to have a second conversation with the family as they left the supermarket with their shopping as we checked over their sheet and gave the children their reward. Standing at the door all day long also meant that we had a chance to talk to those just walking by and to have a second conversation with anyone who came back out after touring the shop to ask them how they felt about the trail.

For those who already have a spiritual inclination it can be treated rather like a labyrinth, as a form of meditation or prayer, with the added bonus that you're ticking off your shopping list for the week at the same time.

Getting agreement for something like this requires some careful negotiation, sometimes involving the head office of a supermarket chain, so it's important to have thought through all the details of how you would like to do this so as to make it as easy as possible for management to say yes to it. It is sometimes worth presenting this as an add-on to their corporate social responsibility programme if they have one, and certainly to point out that it's a good link with the local community as represented by the church, especially if the church is close to the shop in question. It is also a good idea to let the store manager know that you will be doing media publicity for the event and will ensure that the particular store is namechecked as much as possible, and that church congregations will be made aware of how helpful the store has been and may well become new customers as a result!

A spiritual trail using shop windows or a supermarket can be created in any town or village; you just need some courage to approach store owners and managers.

Start with people who you know. Maybe it's the corner shop where you buy your milk or somewhere that you regularly buy clothes. It's easier to have a conversation about this with someone you know, even if it's only a casual shopper/shop worker relationship, and you're more likely to get a positive response if there is already some sort of relationship there.

Begin your creativity from the same place as the shop that you're targeting. If it's a shoe shop start by thinking about Jesus' pierced feet or Mary washing Jesus' feet or Jesus washing the disciples' feet at the Last Supper. Be prepared for some lateral thinking about how you might create that link between the shop and the faith story that you want to tell. If they can see a link, they are more likely to say yes.

Look for ways in which this may benefit the shop. Point out that being part of a trail like this may mean an increase in footfall to their shop, especially if it's in a slightly obscure location. Add in the fact that their shop will feature in all your promotion and that some church folk might be visiting the shop who would normally not go anywhere near it. Let them know that they may feature in any media coverage that would result from the event and that you will be actively issuing press releases as part of the project.

Be prepared for a discussion about how this might work. Part of the process of creating a trail of this kind is the discussion with people about why you're doing this and what your faith means to you. This is just as important as getting the trail set up.

Be open to their interpretation of faith. This is a theme that you will come across time and time again in this book. Engaging with 'the public' about Christian faith requires us to be open to their understanding of this, which is often quite different from ours. This means they may come up with ideas that you don't necessarily agree with, but at least they are engaging in the discussion. The process of doing this is just as important as the end result and in some cases may even be more important.

Things to consider

- How might a retail trail fit in your own locality? What kinds of shops would be available to help and how are they located geographically?
- What's the best theme for your trail? Is this for Lent or Advent or some other form of pilgrimage?
- Think about who might be the best person in your team to approach each shop; it requires a certain amount of courage to ask retailers to get involved with something like this.

- Make sure your art and your signage don't interfere with the overall window display.
- Ensure your signage is clear and allows random passers-by and shoppers to understand and take part easily.

6

Church Festivals

It began with a chance encounter in the city of London, known more as a centre for financial wheeling and dealing rather than as a place of spiritual enlightenment. I happened to be in the capital and had some time to kill and remembered that a friend had installed something in one of the medieval churches that are dotted around the square mile. I sought this out and discovered an ancient service, possibly going back to the early church but certainly in general practice by the Middle Ages, entitled Tenebrae. *Tenebrae* is the Latin for 'darkness' and this immediately appealed to me as someone who relishes the opportunity to explore dark themes in Christian life, especially if this can be combined with some creative use of light. I set about researching this service with a view to creating one as part of the Beyond programme.

What I discovered was that the term 'Tenebrae' can be used to describe all the services of the Triduum (that is, the set of services that are run on the three days from Maundy Thursday through to Easter), as well as being a service itself with its own liturgy. The liturgy centred on a set of six candles that began the service alight and which were gradually extinguished until the service closed in total darkness. It also seemed to be particularly associated with Holy Saturday, a day which had grown in importance to me as the day between Jesus' death on the cross but when the glory of resurrection was yet to come.

While studying for the priesthood I was interested in the relationship between Jesus' humanity and divinity and in particular what this meant for him as he approached death. As human beings we approach death with a variety of attitudes, but the universal truth is that we do not know what lies beyond this life. Religion gives us hope of heaven and eternal life, and I want to affirm that, but ultimately all that we can actually know is that this human life will end. Theological college provoked me to think about what it meant for Jesus to approach the cross in the same way that all humans do, with no expectation of resurrection. Of course, the Gospels tell us that Jesus spoke about being raised again at various points in his ministry but some scholars point out that all of these accounts of Jesus' life were written with hindsight, and that the writers knew that Jesus had been resurrected so may have inserted these quotes or given them more emphasis.

For me, the idea that Jesus went to his death on the cross thinking that this was the end for him made his self-sacrifice even more meaningful, even more of an act of altruism and martyrdom, as he was truly abandoning himself to his fate, the fate that we all will experience. The Tenebrae service was a perfect vehicle to explore this difficult concept, especially if it takes place on Holy Saturday when effectively God is dead. So I began the search for a suitable venue which would evoke thoughts of death and darkness, redolent with the solemnity of the grave and the loss of hope. A place where we could feel the pain the disciples would have felt having seen their leader and teacher die on a cross. A place that reminded us of the women placing Jesus' broken body in a garden tomb and rolling a stone across, sealing him into the darkness.

The answer came in one of the Brighton seafront hotels which I discovered had a set of cellars that were mainly used for storage but one of these could be hired for events. I arranged a site visit and was taken down under the hotel to a dank cavern-like space with a low domed ceiling and enough room for 30–40 people. I asked the hotel manager if we could turn the lights off and was immediately plunged into the kind of absolute inky blackness that is so disorientating that you're not quite sure where you are. It was perfect and so I immediately booked it for the Saturday in April before Easter Sunday and came home to work out what we were going to do in the space.

The only aspect of the service that I knew about was the extinguishing of the six candles and that some friends in a church in London had run a similar event, so I began asking around for an order of service that I could use. Eventually, a document appeared in my inbox with a service that was divided into six sections with liturgy largely comprised of Bible readings. The six sections matched the six candles that would be blown out, and were described as 'shadows'. Each had a title:

1. The Shadow of Betrayal
2. The Shadow of Anguish
3. The Shadow of Treachery
4. The Shadow of Hypocrisy
5. The Shadow of Humiliation
6. The Shadow of Death

Accompanying these sections and the readings were suggested items of music and various ritual actions such as throwing some coins on the ground during the section on betrayal, as a reference to Judas receiving 30 pieces of silver. I wanted to add more performative actions and rituals to this, such that every part of the service would involve all of our senses, and so I began to shape a service around this skeleton, adding in other elements so that attendees would be active participants, not just passive recipients. I was also aware that we'd need some extra light in addition to the candles and therefore planned to use a video projector to show imagery so that we didn't need to use the fluorescent lights installed in the cellar.

On Holy Saturday the six candles were already alight as people entered the cellar, and on the way in they were invited to wash their hands in a bowl of red wine, which set an interesting tone to the service before we'd even begun. Dipping your hands in red wine is an unusual experience and is undertaken with some trepidation and reluctance. Attendees were directed to dry their hands on a large white sheet that was being offered by one of our volunteers. Once everyone had entered and was settled, the sheet was then hung at one end of the cellar to become the projection screen for the imagery of the service, complete with stains from the wine.

The service began with two volunteers laying a low table with a white cloth, plates, glasses, bread and wine so as to evoke the feeling of being present at the Last Supper. On the white sheet we projected images of bread being kneaded and grapes being crushed as further reference to preparations for a meal. The reading was a dramatized version of Matthew 26 describing the preparations for the Last Supper and Jesus' identification of Judas as his betrayer. At the end of it the first candle was extinguished and the volunteers cleared away all the items on the table.

The second shadow began with the placing of a crude pottery vase on the table and imagery on screen of a slow-motion drop of blood falling into water. The reading this time was from Psalm 31, where the psalmist describes being weak with sorrow and grief and rejected like a broken pot, at which point the pot on the table was smashed to smithereens with a large lump hammer. The sound echoed around the cellar and the sudden violence of this action combined with bits of pottery flying around the space introduced a moment of fierce aggression into what had been up to then a silent meditative environment. This was followed with a continuation of the narrative in Matthew when Jesus takes the disciples to the Garden of Gethsemane so that he can pray, but they are unable to stay the course with him due to their tiredness and weakness of will.

The third shadow is about treachery, and the table was cleared of shards of crockery, with the fragments being swept and scattered on the floor. One of the volunteers stepped forward and sat on the table wearing a white shirt with bright red lipstick stains on the collar. Just in case this wasn't visible enough to the congregation, the video screen showed a close-up image of these stains. The reading continued, recounting the episode where Judas betrays Jesus with a kiss, at which point the shirt was placed on the table and we listened to the version of the Des'ree track 'Kissing You' with an overlaid voiceover repeating some of the key phrases from the reading that we already had from another project (see Chapter 2). Once again, the section closed with a candle being extinguished, and the shirt was removed.

The Shadow of Hypocrisy began with the table being laid with a bowl, a jug full of water and a towel. The video screen showed a loop of Pilate washing his hands in a bowl of water, taken from a scene in the film *Jesus Christ Superstar*. A slow drum beat began as we heard a dramatized reading of Pilate asking the crowd to choose between Jesus and Barabbas. As a chorus of 'crucify him' began, the water in the jug was poured into the bowl and I stepped forward to wash my hands in it. I then blew out the next candle and the table was cleared once more, to be set with an unusual crown of thorns. I had wanted this to be made of barbed wire but my research had discovered that barbed wire is only available in bulk and I didn't really want to buy enough wire to fence in a small field in order to make one little crown. So I ended up raiding an overgrown stretch of hedgerow near my house to obtain a length of bramble that I stripped of its leaves and wove into a circlet, taking care to wear a good pair of work gloves to ensure I didn't hurt myself.

On screen we showed a video loop of hand-tools and nails accompanied by a scratching, banging soundtrack as a member of the team read the account of Jesus being stripped and dressed in a purple robe by the Roman soldiers, who then mocked him, hit him and spat on him. After a short pause filled only with the audio, a second team member read from Isaiah 53.

Up until this point there had been no reference to a large wooden cross which was positioned on the floor from the beginning of the service. While these words were being read, a third team member knelt at this cross and, using the same lump hammer that we had used earlier, drove three large nails into the cross at the point where hands and feet would have been placed. The sound echoed around the cavernous cellar, shockingly loud and unsettling, assaulting our ears and disrupting our meditation. This was the prelude to the fifth candle being blown out so that the cellar was slowly becoming gloomier and dark.

The final shadow began with a return to the opening set-up as the table was once again laid with a white cloth, plates and glasses, bread and wine. We watched a short clip from the film *Fight Club* about pain, sacrifice, God and redemption, before the final reading of Jesus' words on the cross, 'My God, my God, why have you forsaken me?' The Bible then tells us that someone offered Jesus a vinegar-filled sponge on the end of a stick. At this point the bread on the table was broken and everyone was invited to take a piece and dip it into the 'wine', which actually was red wine vinegar. The acrid fumes from the chalice and the shock of eating a piece of bread soaked in this caused many people's eyes to water, bringing about an unexpected solidarity with those who saw Jesus die 2,000 years ago.

Once everyone had taken part in 'communion' the final part of the story was read: 'When Jesus had received the wine he said, "It is finished." Then he bowed his head and gave up his spirit.'

Two team members took the white sheet that we had been using as a projection screen and ripped it in half: 'At that moment the curtain of the temple was torn in two from top to bottom.'

I stepped forward and blew out the final candle and at the same time the projector was turned off. For a few moments we sat in the velvety darkness until it was filled with the *strepitus*. This was the 'wild noise' or 'crash' caused by the slamming shut of a large Bible that had lain quietly on the floor throughout the service, unused and unnoticed up to that point. This is meant to represent the thunder and lightning that accompanied Jesus' death on the cross and the breaking open of the graves across the city of Jerusalem as the dead came to life.

Following this crescendo in the darkness everyone sat quietly, contemplating the events of the last 40 minutes, thinking about the story of Good Friday and dwelling on the day between that and Easter day, when God in human form was forsaken by God in heavenly form and what that might mean for each of us. Then we slowly opened the door to the rest of the hotel, letting in a little light so that people could make their way out to the bright lights and noise of the hotel upstairs, where a riotous wedding reception was in full swing, reminding us that daily life continued for most people, unaware of the momentous commemoration of God's salvation of the world that had just taken place below their feet.

Since that first staging of the Tenebrae we have gone back to the hotel cellar a couple more times, and we took the service to a small 800-year-old redundant church, where we were surrounded by medieval murals featuring the murder of Thomas Becket. More recently I've held the service in the church where I am vicar, as part of our Easter pattern of services. On one occasion we finished the service in the dark and then settled down to sleep in the church as our Easter vigil, getting up at dawn for a Eucharist and breakfast. Each time we've run the service I've edited and (hopefully) refined the liturgy, so the order of service we now use is very different from the first one underground in that seafront hotel.

My tradition has always been to hold the service on the evening of Holy Saturday as thematically that is the obvious time to hold it, as that's the day when Jesus' body was lying in the tomb. Some churches hold Tenebrae services on the Wednesday of Holy Week so that it doesn't interrupt the succession of services which begins with the Maundy Thursday Eucharist, Good Friday services of various kinds including walks of witness and a Saturday night vigil with a bonfire and lighting of the Paschal candle. The tradition of Holy Saturday vigils relies on a convention that a day is considered to begin at sunset. This is

when a Jewish sabbath begins, at sunset on a Friday night, and this same thinking has filtered through to the Christian church in a whole range of denominations.

There is a natural human desire to move on as quickly as possible from the darkness and despair of death to the hope and joy of resurrection, but I believe there is value in dwelling on the difficult times as this is so much a part of the human condition. For me the fact that God has experienced the depths of human desolation and grief is a hugely comforting fact of faith which makes all forms of human difficulty easier to bear. To know that God understands our darkest moments because of Jesus' death is something worth focusing on and shouldn't be skipped over just because we can't endure it. Christians are very ready to celebrate the optimism of Easter and this can lead to a glossing over of the sadly real fact that life is often tough. I think it's worth dwelling for a few moments or hours on the grave, to remind us of the importance of Jesus' sacrifice and death and his identification with the struggles that many experience.

I would rather save the resurrection celebration for dawn on Easter day, not only because two of the Gospels specifically state dawn as the time when the women went to the garden tomb to find the stone had been rolled away, but also because it's generally recognized in the western world as the time when a day begins. It's also a magical time of day to be out and about, especially when you live by the beach, although in England in April there's always a high risk that the day will dawn grey and cold and you may not see the sunrise at all.

I've taken dawn Easter services on the beach, including on one occasion with a baptism in the sea. Easter is a traditional time for baptism and the early church used the season of Lent to teach those who wished to become Christians, prior to their baptism with great celebration at Easter. This was the process of catechism, literally of handing down the faith through oral instruction. In its extreme form those to be baptized would be taken into the catacombs in Rome for this instruction, emerging on Easter day for their baptism, clad in white and ready to start a new life in Christ. When I was at theological college, we made a short video about this for one of our academic modules, dressing ourselves in white sheets and reciting the catechism in a reality-style video shot in the dimly lit college boiler room!

I didn't expect anyone to dress in white sheets the morning of our Easter dawn baptism service, although some of us who were due to go into the sea were wearing wetsuits as the English Channel is pretty cold in early April. We combined the service with another church group who had been running dawn services on Easter day for a while and so there was a good gathering of folk at 5.30 a.m. to walk to the beach. I'd already checked that the tide would be a good way out at that time on the day, as the beach is pretty steep at high tide and you only need to take a few steps into the water to get out of your depth. I'd also arranged for a couple of baptism helpers, one of whom was a trained lifeguard, so that no one got drowned rather than just dipped in the water!

The service began with 15 minutes of silence as we sat on the beach and watched the sunrise at 6.10 a.m. I then started an a capella version of 'Alleluia, Alleluia, Give thanks to the risen Lord'. As we sang about Jesus being king of creation and the good news of new life for all, we gave thanks for Jesus' death and resurrection.

We used the narrative of John 21 as the Bible reading for the service; this isn't the first resurrection account which is usually used on Easter day but is a later account, when Jesus appears to the disciples on a beach and helps them to catch an enormous haul of fish. This was a much more appropriate reading for us in our setting and includes the story of Peter putting on his clothes and jumping into the water to be with Jesus, something that I'd always thought was a bit peculiar but which fitted the occasion very well. We split the reading into two halves and began with verses 1–7:

Jesus appeared to his disciples again. It was by the Sea of Galilee. Here is what happened. Simon Peter and Thomas, who was also called Didymus, were there together. Nathanael from Cana in Galilee and the sons of Zebedee were with them. So were two other disciples. 'I'm going out to fish,' Simon Peter told them. They said, 'We'll go with you.' So they went out and got into the boat. That night they didn't catch anything.

Early in the morning, Jesus stood on the shore. But the disciples did not realize that it was Jesus.

He called out to them, 'Friends, don't you have any fish?'

'No,' they answered.

He said, 'Throw your net on the right side of the boat. There you will find some fish.' When they did, they could not pull the net into the boat. There were too many fish in it.

Then the disciple Jesus loved said to Simon Peter, 'It is the Lord!' As soon as Peter heard that, he put his coat on. He had taken it off earlier. Then he jumped into the water. (NIrV)

At this point we stopped the reading and switched to the standard Church of England baptism liturgy, beginning with a prayer and moving into the declarations, asking the candidates whether they turned to Christ, repented of their sins and renounced evil. After signing each candidate with the sign of the cross in holy oil we all joined in an affirmation of our common faith as laid out in the creed. Then came the moment to enter the water.

As expected, it was freezing cold as I waded out accompanied by my two helpers and the three candidates: an asylum seeker from Iraq, a woman from St Luke's who was going forward for ordination and a young mum I had met through the Beach Hut Advent Calendar, who wanted to affirm her new-found faith. Each person placed themselves in my care as I spoke the words: 'I baptize you in the name of the Father, and of the Son, and of the Holy Spirit', and gently lowered them into the waves while the helpers stood behind me to help lift them back up again and to ensure that no one disappeared under the grey-green water.

Each came up out of the water with a huge smile of joy on their face and one punched the sky in exhilaration as they symbolically died under the waters of the English Channel and rose again with a new life ahead of them, filled and inspired by the Holy Spirit. We walked together back up the beach to the waiting congregation as I pronounced words of welcome: 'There is one Lord, one faith, one baptism: by one Spirit we are all baptized into one body. We welcome you into the fellowship of faith; we are children of the same heavenly Father; we welcome you', and the whole beach burst into a round of applause.

The instructions on the order of service that I had prepared then said: 'We share the peace and get changed if necessary!' This was followed by prayers for the candidates, their families and friends, for the church and the world, led by one of my priest colleagues. Then came the second instalment of the reading from John 21, completing the story of Jesus' resurrection appearance on the beach:

> The other disciples followed in the boat. They were towing the net full of fish. The shore was only about 100 yards away. When they landed, they saw a fire of burning coals. There were fish on it. There was also some bread.
>
> Jesus said to them, 'Bring some of the fish you have just caught.' So Simon Peter climbed back into the boat. He dragged the net to shore. It was full of large fish. There were 153 of them. But even with that many fish the net was not torn. Jesus said to them, 'Come and have breakfast.' None of the disciples dared to ask him, 'Who are you?' They knew it was the Lord. Jesus came, took the bread and gave it to them. He did the same thing with the fish. This was the third time Jesus appeared to his disciples after he was raised from the dead. John 21.8–14 (NIrV)

After joining in with 'Sing Hallelujah to the Lord' including the verse 'Jesus is risen from the dead', we gathered around a small fire that was being tended by one of the volunteers to share in a fish barbecue and to hear some poetry about resurrection and new life. Before we shared the food and drink, a kind of fishy take on communion, I lit three candles from the flames of the barbecue fire to give to each of the candidates with the final words from the baptism liturgy:

> You have received the light of Christ;
> walk in this light all the days of your life.
> Shine as a light in the world
> to the glory of God the Father.

With these words we began to share the fish, bread and drink that had been brought to the beach, with the newly baptized candidates acting as servers and helping everyone to take part in this special Easter meal.

I've run other services on the beach, including other baptisms, and they always attract random passers-by. During one service I noticed a middle-aged gentleman pause as he walked past to watch what we were doing before continuing his morning constitutional. Five minutes later he was back and once again paused. Almost imperceptibly he began to shuffle towards us, one step at a time, so slowly that you could hardly notice this gentle progress towards the congregation. As we reached the end of the service, we all stood to sing 'Thine be the Glory' and I noticed he was joining in heartily and clearly knew all the verses. I planned on going over to speak to him when we finished, but as soon as the hymn ended, he was gone, almost as though he had never been there.

Holding services in open public spaces allows people to choose their level of participation without any fear of being drawn in or confronted in any way. My friend Milton Jones tells a joke asking why Christianity is like a helicopter – because if you get too close you'll be drawn into the rotors/rotas. The church has done a good job in modern times of helping people understand that attending on Sundays requires some sort of openness to faith; gone are the days when it didn't matter if the people in the pews believed in God. But what about those who wish to find out about faith? How do they do that without already showing some sort of allegiance to the Christian club? I often bemoan the fact that church has become a place for people who know what they believe rather than a place for people to find out about belief. Taking our worship into a public space does away with any requirement to commit and makes us more open to inquisitive onlookers.

It's challenging to do this, as once out in the open you begin to understand that so much of what we do in church is a bit weird. Singing together is not a very common practice for most people other than at gigs or football matches or if you join a community choir. Standing up and sitting down in unison, turning to face in certain directions, following the lead of someone wearing funny clothes, greeting total strangers as we share the peace, sitting and closing our eyes together in prayer, eating little slivers of wafer and sipping drops of wine and calling it a meal ... Taking these ritual actions into a public space can act as a witness to casual observers, especially if there is some sort of explanation, but can also be viewed as an oddity which is anachronistic to a modern, post-Christendom society. Moving 'ordinary' church out into a public space also makes those of us who curate these services, and take part week in and week out, think more deeply about what we're doing. Every time I've taken a service in a public space it prompts feelings of nervousness, exhilaration and uncertainty, which moves me out of my usual Sunday-morning comfort zone, which is no bad thing as it helps to banish the complacency that can so easily become a part of regular church life.

Things to consider

- There is a richness of tradition in the ancient rituals of the church, which are ripe for re-invention and can be a great source of inspiration for new ideas.
- If you are looking to re-invent old practices, don't be constricted by the ways these have been implemented before. Use the core of the idea to launch you into new areas of artistic endeavour.
- Be prepared to allow artistic rituals to develop and change as you repeat them.
- Think about taking some of the regular church services out into other locations, and be open to how these might change as a result.

7

Light Events

Light held a fascination for me long before I associated it with religion, and I suspect that we all have some sort of affinity with light, whether it's wondering at the gorgeous colours of a sunset, marvelling at the moon and stars at night, gazing into the flickering light of a fire, watching a firework display or being dazzled by light effects at concerts or festivals. Alongside the daily use of light in our homes and workplaces to help us see, there are plenty of opportunities to experience light as something mesmerizing and spiritual, beautiful and inspiring, whether in a natural setting or artificially generated by science and technology. It's no wonder that light has a place in every religion, especially during the dark days of winter or in the hidden recesses of dark church buildings.

Advent is the time in the Christian calendar when we have a special focus on light, and I've written in Chapter 1 about the Beach Hut Advent Calendar and the importance of light as part of this countdown to Christmas. But there is value in focusing on light in itself, not as part of a seasonal topic, and this has been a fruitful theme for artistic and spiritual events throughout the lifetime of Beyond. This was one area where my work life and my passion for God came together and resulted in something as close to a worship service as we've ever come.

I've been a priest since 1988 but only a full-time vicar since 2010. Up to that point I did a proper job, if you can call working in television a proper job. I worked in quite a niche part of the broadcast TV industry creating branding, logos and graphics for broadcasters, production companies and large corporates like Disney, Sky and the BBC. Throughout 20 years in this business

I got to work with many brilliant creative people, helping them to realize the designs they had dreamed up using my skills as a producer, account manager and brand strategist. The last five years of this career I ran my own consultancy and it was while doing this that I found myself working with an artist who shared my passion for the spiritual aspects of light.

Early in 2008 I was asked to redesign the broadcast branding for the UEFA Champions League and decided to ask a design agency to help with this, as I knew that the creative director was a huge football fan as well as an accomplished designer. We were given a small budget to aid us in producing some visuals for the pitch and before long I found myself in a smoke-filled photographic studio with a 1-metre-high metal cut-out of the famous Champions League starball twirling on a piece of nylon while an artist called Chris Levine fired lasers at it, creating all sorts of amazing light effects.

Chris and I became friends that day as we talked about light and the way he used it, and in particular lasers, to help him in his meditation practice. I was just in the process of setting up Beyond and one of the events I already had in mind was to produce some sort of Advent light service. When it came to actually planning this, Chris was the obvious person to call and he graciously consented to come along with a production manager and bring a selection of his light artworks.

So we had some raw material for creating a light event but what would it contain? As a team we discussed what we would like to achieve with this event and came up with a general objective for the evening: 'To take people on a journey from darkness to light, symbolic of moving from death to life, ignorance to knowledge, sin to grace, bad to good and so on.'

To help create the right atmosphere we decided to start with candlelight, and everyone would be given a lit candle as they entered the venue and be invited to sit at any one of a number of tables set up with black cloths on them. We thought it would be good to start at first principles by saying something about what light is. Fortunately, one of the people who had attended some of our events was a Professor of Physics from Sussex University, so we asked him to say a few words about the nature of light and its importance to life, the universe and everything.

Following this introduction, we thought we'd ask everyone to blow out their candles so that the room was plunged into darkness while we listened to some quotes about light, and then began a discussion in the dark. We wondered how chatting with strangers in the dark would be different and thought it would create a great counterpoint when finally we asked people to experience light. This was when we would switch on a whole variety of light installations to let people really explore and appreciate it. This would be the core of the evening, time just to have an experience of light without any guidance or direction, to allow people to come into contact with different forms of light and to wonder and enjoy it.

On the Sunday of the event, we had hired a local studio theatre which had fantastic blackout facilities and Chris turned up with his magic lights. These included a number of Laserpods – a device he had invented that was being described by others as the noughties equivalent of a lava lamp, as it produced random light patterns by firing three small lasers at a slowly revolving crystal. He also brought what he called a 'blipvert', although the technical name for this is a 'peripheral imaging LED'. It's a vertically mounted strip light that flickers at a particular frequency and has been coded with an image or a message, in this case the word 'LOVE'. You can only see the image out of the corner of your eye as you glance at the light, something I never seemed to get the hang of, but I know others could see the word quite well. He also brought a beautiful little Perspex cube with red LED lights embedded in it in the shape of a cross.

Alongside this I had recently seen a TV programme about light and its use in art, which had given me some ideas for other light installations. In particular I was really keen to create a light tunnel that I had seen on the programme, although there had been no explanation about how it was made, so I had to invent my own. I used Keynote (the Mac version of PowerPoint) to produce a simple outline animation of a white oval on a black background that slowly rotated and changed shape until it became a dia-

mond and then looped back again. Hooking this up to a video projector in a dark room full of smoke created a morphing, fluid tunnel of light which widened as it beamed across the room with the smoke creating abstract flowing patterns on the 'wall' of the tunnel.

I sourced a number of laser pens in both green and red, along with faceted crystals in various sizes to fire these at, ranging from an old Victorian doorknob down to little diamond-shaped Christmas decorations. For good measure I also got hold of a disco ball and some powerful torches. All of this was packed into crates and boxes and bags ready to be taken to the theatre to set everything up. As with any hire of a space like a theatre or a pub, we didn't have a great deal of set-up time so needed to be pretty efficient when installing the various pieces of equipment, but we were also inventing things on the spot, as many of the artworks had to be tailored to the space once we were in it, so we needed time to experiment and adapt as we went along.

Overall, there were ten of us setting up and we arranged to get into the venue two hours before the start time and worked in small groups on different aspects of the installation so as to maximize our time and efficiency. Chris set to installing his proper light art and I had brought two projectors for the tube animation so that we could set up two different light tunnels. Laser pens were mounted above head height, so that they couldn't shine into people's eyes and cause any damage, and crystals were suspended on fishing line. We had a third projector hooked up to a computer with various title slides and the audio clips embedded in them so that we didn't have to run a separate set of audio kit. This is generally how I do all our events as it keeps things simple and helps to make sure everything runs smoothly.

At opening time, a hundred people turned up and there was quite a buzz around the tables as people took their seats, helped by the fact that the theatre bar was open and most attendees brought drinks in with them. The ambience felt like a club as people chatted in the light of the candles they had brought in with them. After a brief introduction we moved into the presentation from the professor about the nature of light and then asked everyone to blow out their candles and all other lights in the theatre were extinguished.

Absolute hush descended on the gathering as we listened to the booming voice of Sir John Gielgud reciting from the King James Bible:

> And God said, Let there be light: and there was light. And God saw the light, that it was good: and God divided the light from the darkness. And God called the light Day, and the darkness he called Night. (Genesis 1.3–5a)

There then followed some further quotes about light from other parts of the Bible, along with some poetry, and this led into the discussion time, when we asked them to think about three questions:

- How do you feel in the dark?
- What do you feel you can say in the dark that you can't in the light?
- Do you feel nearer to God in the dark or the light?

Initially people were a little reluctant to speak out in the dark but gradually discussions began in whispered tones and the noise in the room grew as people became more confident about speaking to strangers in this unusual environment. We all felt there was something liberating about chatting in darkness because of the anonymity and the inability to be put off by seeing the look on the faces of our companions.

While this was going on we were surreptitiously fogging up the room so that the light installations would be at their most effective. Unfortunately, smoke machines are quite noisy as they pump out smoke with a whooshing noise, which threatened to interrupt the flow of the conversations going on around the room. But fortunately the discussions were going so well that hardly anyone noticed. After five or six minutes I called the discussions to a close and explained what would happen next. Various light effects would gradually be switched on and everyone was invited to get up from their seats (safely, as the room was still quite dark) and to simply experience the wonder of light; to wander around the different installations, interacting with them if they wished, and just allow themselves to be wowed by this everyday element of our lives which we so often take for granted.

Slowly people began to get up and hesitantly approach the various light artworks. Some families had brought children and these led the way in playing with the light, stepping in and out of the light tunnels, reaching out to touch the red laser needles that emanated from the Laserpods, which seemed so solid as they slowly moved through the murky atmosphere. Gradually people became bolder and the silence was replaced with little gasps of awe as 'LOVE' appeared in their peripheral vision, or there were chuckles as people found themselves stepping over beams of light that seemed like barriers as they were so solid-looking in the midst of the darkness. Others just gazed at the LED cross or watched the beams of laser light criss-cross the space above their heads.

We let this run for around 20 minutes so that everyone got a chance to experience the full variety of the installations, before inviting people to return to their seats for the conclusion of the event. As we had Chris Levine with us and he was so experienced with light, I interviewed him about his work and why light was such a spiritual element for him. He explained that he meditated for up to two hours every day and that laser light was an important aid to him in this. Naturally occurring light is generally multi-frequency (i.e. we all know that 'white' light is made up of a spectrum of colours), whereas lasers are highly concentrated single frequencies of light and are therefore pure colour. Chris also explained that certain frequencies of light resonate with us as human beings and can help to engender a sense of calm and peace. He uses this understanding of light and the technology he has mastered to help him achieve a meditative state that he describes as spiritual and which I would describe as drawing closer to God.

We finished with a short question-and-answer session where most of the contributions were expressions of thankfulness for the journey from light to dark that evening. As one person said: 'We made the journey from darkness to light, from ignorance to enlightenment, from sorrow to joy, and we were reminded of the wonder of God and that he is light and in him is no darkness at all.' These were almost the exact words we had used in the objective we had set for the evening.

This really worked as a hybrid between an art installation, an exhibition and a service, as those of us in church circles understand that term. I wouldn't describe it exactly as worship but there were elements in this which were on nodding acquaintance with the idea of worship and there were certainly prayerful moments during the evening. This basic structure then formed the basis for other events themed on light in other settings.

One of the most memorable was taking the idea to Greenbelt one August bank holiday. I was beginning to get involved in the worship programme through running the Sunday-morning Eucharist and I thought the light event would work well as part of the worship programme. The festival was held at Cheltenham racecourse in those days and there were two or three indoor venues dedicated to alternative worship which could be blacked out and were generally used for multimedia events. I bid for a slot and was accepted as part of the worship programme, not realizing this would bring us into conflict with Greenbelt health and safety.

In filling in the long and complicated risk assessment I noted that the venue couldn't be fully blacked out as, for example, people needed to see to move around and fire exits needed to be well lit. On top of that I was informed that the venue had a smoke alarm and that if it went off it meant evacuating the whole building, stopping at least half a dozen other activities that would be going on at the same time. There then followed a long negotiation around the possibility of isolating the fire alarms in that one room so that we could use our smoke machines. Eventually this was agreed as an exception just for us, so I began collecting resources to make this event spectacular.

Chris Levine agreed that I could borrow an artwork he'd created called 'Free the Beam'. It consisted of a 1.5-metre-wide acrylic disk that housed nearly 40 Laserpods. The whole contraption was mounted on a stand and beamed a blizzard of red laser lights horizontally out from the disk like an enormous spiky porcupine of light. I also approached a neon artist I knew in Brighton who had been making 2-metre-high neon crosses using painted wood panels from old fairground rides, and he agreed to let me have four crosses for the installation.

I got to the festival with a van full of stuff including tents, cooking gear and enough camping equipment to satisfy the needs of a whole troop of scouts. After pitching tents and securing the van with all the kit, I went to talk to the organizers about access to the venue and our set-up time, only to be told that the alarms would not be turned off for us and we'd just have to manage. I knew that lasers in a semi-dark room with no smoke wouldn't be visible at all so it began to look as though Beyond wouldn't be running a light worship space after all. Despondently I headed back to the campsite to tell the rest of the team the bad news.

I was up early the next day feeling sorry for myself but still wondering if there was something we could do to salvage our event. The ever-present cold morning mist on the campsite sparkled in the dawn's early light, turning everything into a glistening, radiant vista of cobwebs and dewdrops and lighting up the steam from the kettle I was boiling for the first hot drink of the day. Steam! Mist! There was the answer to our problem with the smoke. An idea had popped into my head to save the event. As soon as it was reasonable to make a call, I phoned some of the team who were on their way to join us, to ask them to stop at a garden centre and pick up half a dozen plant sprayers. We would go ahead with our worship event and make the lasers visible by misting in front of them.

The next day we set up the event just as we had planned, except that in front of each laser installation were one or two volunteers with plant misters at the ready to spray onto the laser beams whenever someone approached. The randomness of the mist that was created and the coolness of the spray on a hot summer afternoon brought a completely different dimension to the event which we could never have planned, not to mention the odd bonus rainbow that appeared. It wasn't the same as doing it in the blacked-out theatre but God isn't the same in every situation. God speaks to us in different ways according to our circumstance, our background and mood and the setting we're in. That's what's so wonderful about creating artistic ways to encounter God – it will almost always be different for each person, in each setting.

Each time we run an event like this is an opportunity to refine, add, edit and augment it, and as this was the first time we had run this in a worshipful context I felt confident to add prayers to it, including this one:

Light of the world,
Shine on us,
Fill our hearts
with the gift of your presence.
Enlighten us,
Fill our worship
with joy and wonder.
Illumine us,
Fill our lives with your radiance,
That our earthly walk
May reflect your holiness
Through Jesus Christ our Lord
Amen.

The biggest challenge in relation to the robustness of theology and relationship to orthodoxy of our work in this field came when I was invited to contribute to the Leicester Diocese Clergy conference. I was asked to present something about the work of Beyond to the 200–300 clergy and staff attending a three-day conference and to give them a sample of a Beyond experience in the form of a light service. Previously I had only ever run events for members of the public but this was going to be to an audience of theologically trained professionals, including Arch-deacons, Cathedral staff and Bishops, as well as some academic theologians who were also speaking at the conference! I couldn't worry about it too much as I have often said I am not a theo-logian, I'm a practitioner, and I just hope that the Holy Spirit keeps my practice theologically sound.

The conference involved a presentation on the work of Beyond and the kinds of events we had been running up to that point. I was also asked to run a break-out workshop using one of our sessions entitled 'GIFT', as a way for clergy to explore their gifts in relation to their ministry. But the most significant request was to help all of the conference attendees experience the light event, both as a service in the main conference hall but also in the chapel attached to the conference centre.

I realized I required more than the little amateur smoke machine I'd bought for our original event and that I'd need a lot more than half a dozen Laserpods. After ascertaining that I had a small budget to play with that would allow me to hire some kit, I followed up with a quick call to Chris Levine, which elicited a promise to lend me once again 'Free the Beam', and this time I could let him have a fee. By now I had developed a light kit with crates full of all the stuff I could use to mount an installation like this.

The great thing about doing this as a residency at a conference centre was that I could set it up as a semi-permanent installation in the chapel, which was the venue for morning and evening prayer every day. It also gave me a chance to chat with people who had tried out the light experience and get feedback about how it made them feel and whether we could improve it at all.

The main event was a full presentation of the work of Beyond up to that point, which concluded with a shortened version of the light experience. It was interesting to move from a 'lecture' into a time of sensory encounter and at first it was hard to get a room full of clergy to 'play' with light. I wished we'd had some of those children who'd attended the first event to help warm things up! But slowly people threw off their inhibitions and began to move around the room, stepping in and out of the light tunnel and reaching out to try and touch the spikes of laser light from the various pieces of apparatus.

The reaction to the work was interesting as it was pretty universally acknowledged to be inspiring, thought-provoking and meditative and gave those who attended a different outlook on the relationship between God and light. But there was some push-back on whether anything like this was possible in a parish situation or for a typical church. I had lots of discussions about the relationship between Catholic tradition in church, using incense, candles and stained glass, and the more performative forms of evangelical worship with bands on stage, lighting rigs and stage effects. It seems to me that these are all pointing towards the possibility of creating similar light experiences; we just need to help those who run churches to open their minds to the possibilities.

I had another opportunity to experiment with light as a source of spiritual enlightenment at a weekend in Belfast curated by Pete Rollins of pyrotheology fame. I planned on attending and asked Pete if there was anything I could do to contribute, mentioning light as a current interest of mine and wondered if that might fit. He embraced this and allocated me a small room in the conference centre where we were all meeting, and so I set off for Belfast with one of our team and my smoke machine, some Laserpods I had bought from Chris Levine, a projector and laptop and my laser pointers and crystals.

It didn't take long to turn the tiny cupboard I'd been allocated into a chapel of light. I blocked the window with some card, hid the smoke machine in the corner on the floor and set up a little Laserpod 'altar' and a green laser beam firing at a crystal on a thread at picture-rail level. We even managed a mini tunnel of light although there wasn't really the space for this. The room worked really well as a quiet meditative space for individuals who wanted to get away for a few minutes' peace or to pray. The one thing that was lacking was some sort of gentle audio to help fill the silence; this would have to be added to the kit list for the next time.

I also got a chance to talk about our work and the creation of the event, and found myself closing with the following adapted quotation from Ephesians 5:

You were in the dark before,
but now God has given you light.
Live like people who have the light.
People who have the light do what is good and right and true.
So learn what pleases God.
Have no part in the empty things people do in the dark.
Show them that they are wrong.
It is a shame even to talk about the things they do in secret.
But when the light shines on something, it can be seen.
For light makes everything visible.

Light exposes evil intentions.
So it is said, `Wake up, you who are asleep!
Rise from death.
Christ will give you light.'
Ephesians 5.8–14 (Worldwide English New Testament)

So this concept was evolving from being a 'happening', to an experience, an ambient installation and almost a form of worship. It was time to turn it into a full act of worship.

The International Ecumenical Fellowship were holding a symposium in Brighton and had heard about Beyond and contacted me to ask if I could help them with some creative worship. The initial idea was to do a dawn service on the beach, travelling down through a secret tunnel that ran from the symposium venue through the cliffs east of Brighton, which really got my creative juices flowing as I started to think about ways to fire lasers along the tunnel and then develop ideas around spiritual journeying. Unfortunately, this turned out not to be possible as the tunnel was unsafe, so I began to make other plans based around some form of light service.

The service was to be held in the Meeting House at Sussex University, a Basil Spence-designed building that was built immediately after his famous work on Coventry Cathedral. It's a circular building with walls that are punctured with hundreds of small squares of coloured stained glass. The principal requirement from the IEF was for a communion service, but they were very happy to incorporate elements from the light events and so I put together a liturgy for the service, which began in a similar way to the original light event with everyone being given a lit candle and an introduction about the nature of light.

This then moved into confession as we acknowledged that we often prefer darkness to light (John 3), and the candles were extinguished. It wasn't possible to black out the chapel so people were invited to close their eyes to put themselves into darkness and to listen to the Taizé chant *Lux Mundi* (light of the world). This led into a short time of prayer for those places, people and situations of darkness in the world. Finally, the congregants were invited to open their eyes and come into the light. We all stood and as presiding minister, I initiated the peace and all were encouraged to share a sign of peace and to discover the various light installations around the chapel that had been switched on while their eyes were closed. Mostly these consisted of video projections as the chapel was too light for any lasers to be effective at this point.

The main reading for the service was from the Gospel of John, chapter 1, finishing at verse 14, which we all said together: 'The Word became flesh and made his dwelling among us. We have seen his glory, the glory of the one and only Son, who came from the Father, full of grace and truth' (NIV).

This then led us into the Eucharist using the simple words of institution from 1 Corinthians 11, in recognition that this was an ecumenical gathering and should avoid any one particular set of liturgical words. As people came forward to receive bread and wine, they could also collect a glowstick to take back to their place. The service then concluded with a prayer based on the words from Ephesians 5. At the close of the prayer everyone was invited to break light together as a symbol of taking light with us

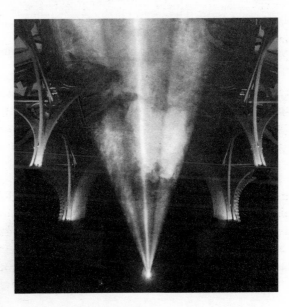

to all the different churches and congregations across the world that were represented in the room. My experience of running a light event for the first-ever Beyond Advent combined with an understanding of the sacramental possibilities of light gained through a Christmas Eve beach hut (see Chapter 1) brought these two concepts together to create a powerful worship service that would fit any church setting without too much extra work.

The culmination of this journey from dark to light was a complete Eucharist of Light for the Grace community in Ealing just before the pandemic lockdown of 2020. This featured all the usual light effects we'd developed with added input from the Leonard Cohen track, 'You Want It Darker', which includes the lyrics:

> A million candles burning
> For the help that never came
> …
> *Hineni, hineni*
> (Leonard Cohen and Patrick Leonard, Columbia Records)

Hineni is Hebrew for 'Here I am', which felt appropriate as part of a time of confession. The service included a Sanctus, breaking bread and blessing wine and sharing these as well as breaking light, and concluded with an official Anglican post-communion prayer:

> Almighty Father,
> whose Son our Saviour Jesus Christ
> is the light of the world:
> may your people,
> illumined by your word and sacraments,
> shine with the radiance of his glory,
> that he may be known,
> worshipped, and obeyed
> to the ends of the earth;
> for he is alive and reigns, now and for ever.
> **Amen**

We had moved from an art event in a studio theatre to a proper church service in a proper church building after a journey which took this concept to the beach, a conference centre, a cupboard in Belfast, a university chapel and finally into a church.

I built up expertise (and crates of equipment) through doing this but you don't need to be an expert in lasers to set up an event on light for yourself. You can start simply with candles in coloured jars, a torch set up behind a stained-glass window or a few cheap sets of Christmas lights from the pound shop. Lava lamps and fibre-optic night lights are readily available very cheaply these days. An awful lot can be achieved with a video projector and a laptop; just think differently about how these might be used. Turn the projector on its side so that the frame matches a blank shape on a wall, experiment with creating your own animations using PowerPoint to animate moving points of light. You don't need a smoke machine, as incense not only creates great clouds of smoke but also adds a holy fragrance to the environment. Laser pens are not as readily available as they used to be due to safety concerns and irresponsible use of them on the football terraces, but Laserpods can be bought online and there's a whole plethora of domestic laser party-lights available these days at very reasonable prices.

I have made a lot of use of glowsticks and the concept of breaking light together has been quite important as a quasi-sacramental act, but I have come to realize that there are environmental consequences to this. Glowsticks are a combination of plastic and glass containing a chemical which is an irritant if you get it on your skin. It's not possible to recycle these as it's a combined product and I don't think it's responsible for us to be using these unless someone invents an eco-friendly version.

There are many references to light in the Bible and in much of the official liturgy produced by every church denomination. Jesus also had quite a lot to say about light, not only describing himself as the light of the world but also telling us that we are the light of the world and that we shouldn't hide that light under a basket.

Just remember:

> This, in essence, is the message we heard from Christ and are passing on to you: God is light, pure light; there's not a trace of darkness in him.
>
> If we claim that we experience a shared life with him and continue to stumble around in the dark, we're obviously lying through our teeth – we're not *living* what we claim. But if we walk in the light, God himself being the light, we also experience a shared life with one another, as the sacrificed blood of Jesus, God's Son, purges all our sin.

1 John 1.5–7 (*The Message*)

Things to consider

- Working with 'proper' artists is inspirational and enlightening; let them do their thing without too much interference.
- Artists need to make a living so, if possible, pay them for their involvement.
- Be open to changing your ideas if the specific location is problematic.
- Consider the environmental impact of your artwork, especially with light as this involves energy usage and potentially non-recyclable resources.
- Lasers only really work in dark, 'foggy' environments so plan accordingly.
- Make sure any installation using lasers is safe and cannot shine directly into anyone's eyes.

8

Folk Tradition

There are certain church seasons or festivals which live on in folk memory even though our society these days is mostly secular. There are the obvious big events such as Christmas and Easter that shape the whole of the calendar year for Western society, and there is still residual memory about other church anniversaries, such as Lent being a time for giving up things and that pancake day marks the start of this, or harvest being an opportunity to celebrate nature. But there are other dates in the church calendar that are less well connected to faith, and these offer an opportunity for revitalization as part of our church mission.

In recent years there has been an explosion in the UK of the folk celebration of Halloween, which has largely been shunned by the church because of its connotations of evil. I believe that all things are redeemed by the work of the cross and this is true of Halloween, which has its roots in the Christian tradition of All Hallows and All Saints. Beyond has sought to reclaim this festival through a number of creative events that have also led to the development of a Halloween initiative at the church that I serve.

Our first attempt to engage with this season was called a Soul Celebration and was intended as an exploration of mortality, our souls and the relationship of these to the concept of heaven. I had been inspired by images of hundreds of floating lanterns that feature as part of the Chinese Hungry Ghost festival, which is usually held in July. I wondered if pumpkins floated and as soon as they started appearing in the shops prior to Halloween I bought one and tried it out in the bath. Success! It did float quite well even when it was just a complete pumpkin, so I figured it would sail even better once it had been hollowed out.

At the west end of Hove is Hove Lagoon, an artificial shallow lake used for windsurfing lessons, canoeing classes and sailing model boats. This would be perfect for floating pumpkins so I approached the surf club there to ask if we could hire their club-house for a couple of hours on the night of Halloween and they said yes and that they would open the bar for us as well. We decided we wanted to divide the evening into two halves: the first half would focus on mortality, which we knew would be a bit depressing, but the second half would be a journey to a place of light and joy.

For the first section I put together a series of timelapse videos of fruit and vegetables rotting and going mouldy, which were projected in a loop onto one of the walls of the clubhouse, which was very dimly lit, with just enough light for people to buy drinks at the bar. I welcomed everyone and opened with verses from Genesis 3:

[God said to Adam,] 'Cursed is the ground because of you; through painful toil you will eat of it all the days of your life. It will produce thorns and thistles for you, and you will eat the plants of the field. By the sweat of your brow you will eat your food until you return to the ground, since from it you were taken; for dust you are and to dust you will return.' Genesis 3.17b–19 (NIV)

I then recited the committal from the funeral service before one of the team read the poem 'Death Lib' by Steve Turner. Then we asked people to reflect on how much they owned and try to make an estimate of their net worth and write this figure on a Beyond cheque that we had created. People were also asked to consider what they might like to write if they had a chance to draw up their own obituary. Once everyone was done, I took the cheques and burnt them in a metal bowl, signifying that we come into the world with nothing and leave the world with nothing. To emphasize this everyone was then invited to receive an ash cross on their forehead as though this were an Ash Wednesday service, and to leave the bar with the words 'Remember that you are dust and to dust you will return' fresh in their memory.

On leaving the clubhouse, everyone was given a flower and invited to follow a light trail that ran along the edge of the lagoon for about 100 metres, guiding them to the second location, which was a pavilion set at one corner of the lagoon. In marked contrast to the gloom of the first location, this was a place of light and colour, with joyful music and the words 'Welcome Home' emblazoned on the building in silver lettering. Everyone was given a glass of fizz and another video projection loop of flowers bursting into bloom ran on the side of the building. Ranged along the floor beneath this was a whole host of pumpkins into which one of our team had managed to carve a Bible verse from the book of Revelation 21:

> God's home is now among his people! He will live with them, and they will be his people. God himself will be with them. He will wipe every tear from their eyes, and there will be no more death or sorrow or crying or pain. All these things are gone forever. Revelation 21.3b–4 (NLT)

Participants were given another piece of paper to replace the cheque they had written on before and asked to write down things that gave them a taste of heaven. The responses were universally positive and included: 'Seeing things as they truly are'; 'Affection from a child'; 'Seeing a beautifully formed wave up close': 'Snow sparkling in the sun'; 'Being truthful with everybody'.

The 'heavenly' location was filled with chatter and laughter, such a contrast to the gloomy, silent, downbeat atmosphere of the clubhouse. After 15 minutes of people writing, talking to each other and watching the videos, I called them all together and we read the verse carved into the pumpkins before inviting everyone to pick up a pumpkin and set it afloat on the lagoon. As these all started to drift slowly across the water, which was mercifully calm that night, I read out this blessing based on some words by John O'Donohue:

> Go gently on your voyage, beloved.
> Slip away with the ebb tide,

rejoice in a new sunrise.
May the moon make a path across the sea for you,
the Son provide a welcome.
May the earth receive you
and the fire cleanse you
as you go from our love
into the presence of Love's completeness.

In France there is a festival called *Nuit Blanche* (White Night) when all sorts of light events, art installations, exhibitions and shops stay open late into the night as a way of lightening the mood of the city as the nights draw in and the days get shorter. The idea for this began at a festival in Helsinki and has spread to other cities including, for a short while, Brighton. The Brighton version of *Nuit Blanche* was scheduled to coincide with Halloween as a night with similar themes, and we thought we would also pick up that same theme for an event of our own. We called it Grey Night, as the date we chose was between the citywide white-night festival and Halloween itself, and grey is the halfway point between light and dark, white and black.

Our aim this time was to explore the complex space between sinners and saints and for our venue we were able to secure All Saints church in Hove, which is a cathedral-like parish church stacked full of images and statues of saints. As people entered the church they were invited to stroll around looking at the imagery and in particular to look at a set of posters we had created of various saints and their stories, some of whom were distinctly eccentric. Each person had a little pack of different-coloured sticky notes and the idea was to put a green note on posters that you thought were true and a pink one on false stories, introducing the idea of true and false, black and white and the grey area that sits between these extremes.

The posters included St Kevin, who was standing with his hands folded in prayer at the beginning of Lent when a blackbird settled on him and laid an egg in his arms. Not wishing to disturb the incubating egg, St Kevin remained in that position for the whole of Lent, being fed by the blackbird until the egg hatched at Easter. We also featured St Denis, who is one of a select group of saints called cephalophores. These are saints who had their heads chopped off but then picked them up and carried them around; in the case of St Denis he did this while continuing to preach a sermon on repentance. Many of the stories of the saints are fantastical, but no less true in that they illustrate something about the nature of faith which can be helpful to a believer.

The space also illustrated the dichotomy between dark and light, as the west end of the church featured a large black circular tarpaulin laid on the floor and at the other end was a similar white circle. In the middle of the black circle was a cubic plinth and placed on it was a model skull, eerily lit from inside and seemingly preaching to us via a recording of an American megachurch pastor shouting hellfire and damnation and telling the congregation that 'God hates some of you, personally hates you!'

I was surprised to find this kind of preaching online as I thought that bludgeoning people into the kingdom was not a very postmodern way of behaving and I can't believe that it works. I don't want people to follow Jesus because they're scared and I don't think it's an appropriate way to speak to people today. For me it belongs to the kind of preaching which starts by assuming that the hearers are filthy rotten sinners and know that they are and therefore need God. I think that most people these days believe themselves to be good and do their best, and so preaching or speaking of God in this way starts from a false premise. I think it's best to start with concepts and values that people can identify with and match those to the values of the kingdom of God rather than start from a negative position about all of humanity.

The attendees were also surprised to be preached at by a skull, especially as we made them stand around and listen to the whole seven minutes of audio. Scattered around the black circle were small card cut-outs of people with 'God hates ...' written on them. We asked everyone to pick up a figure and add to it what they thought God might hate about them and to keep this with them as we followed a light path to the east end of the church and the white circle. En route were various Bible quotes placed on the floor about saints and an explanation from the Common Worship companion book *Saints on Earth*:

In using the word 'saint' to describe those commemorated in the Holy Days of the *Common Worship* calendar we are using it as a shorthand term. From a biblical perspective there is no difficulty in the use of the word, since it simply signifies those who are 'in Christ' – being dead is not a necessary part of the equation!

In his epistles Paul uses the word extensively to refer to his fellow believers. But in common understanding 'saints' are exceptionally holy individuals who have been officially canonized by the Church. Yet, unlike the Roman Catholic Church, the Church of England has no machinery for doing this. Indeed, the very idea of the Church taking it upon itself to bestow 'sainthood' on some of its departed members is one that many Anglicans would find very difficult to accept. Even King Charles I, the only post-Reformation 'saint' to get into the 1662 Prayer Book (until removed in the nineteenth century), was never referred to as such, merely as a 'martyr'.

The Bible references reinforced the idea that saints are all those who love God; that is, every one of us ordinary Christian believers.

At the end of this journey from dark to light we arrived at the white circle, which also had cardboard cut-out people scattered over it, but these had the words 'God loves...' written on them, and once again participants were invited to complete this phrase from their perspective. The figures had slits cut in them so they could be slotted together to form a three-dimensional person that could be made to stand just in front of the altar of the church. The figures formed a small crowd of people standing on the altar steps, where a beautiful pair of glittering silver angel wings had been placed. These had been made by one of our team for the Beach Hut Advent Calendar and were perfectly placed to create a selfie photo moment. Everyone took a turn to stand in front of the wings creating a silvery image of themselves as an angel, complete with shining halo.

Once we had a complete set of angel photos, we progressed to one final ritual act, which we performed together. The large white circular cloth was hoisted up from the floor and carried to the back to be laid over the black circle and the black plinth, now vacant as the skull had been removed. Laid out on a table nearby were a number of plastic cups, and written on them were various statements telling us things that we sometimes think about ourselves or others, factors that can greatly affect how we behave. Cups with negative statements contained black paint and those with white paint displayed positive phrases. Each person was invited to take a cup and pour the contents into the centre of the plinth, which was sitting under the white sheet. As the black merged with the white and the white mixed with the black, we saw all of our pristine categories of saints, sinners and everything else, beautifully merge into one with streaks of grey between the streams of black or white. We saw our boundaries, our classifications and definitions rolling and blending into one large grey mass.

Because the plinth was underneath the cloth, the paint followed the path of least resistance, which led to it overflowing

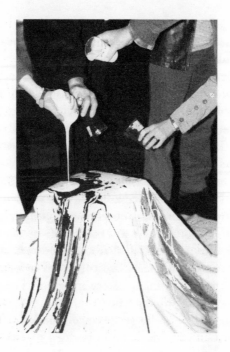

down the four sides of the cube but not the corners. Once everyone had added as much paint as they wanted, four of us lifted the cloth up, keeping it as tight and flat as possible and laid it on the floor exposing the significance of the ensuing grey puddle that miraculously revealed itself to have taken the abstract form of a cross streaked with black, white and grey.

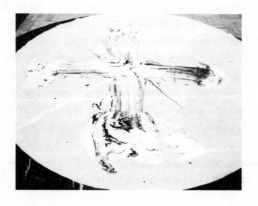

Once the event was over, we attempted to transport the abstract cross on its white tarpaulin to another location so that the paint could dry and it might then become a permanent artwork, but the challenges of moving a large cloth with quite deep pools of liquid paint proved too difficult as the paint continued to run and obliterate the cross form which had been such a revelation. We so easily forget the grace that infuses our Christian faith and wipes away all our dark attributes and actions leaving us as white as snow.

The analogy between dark and light is not a perfect one when described as black and white, with the overtones of racism that can be implied when using those colours, although there is an aspect of certainty and separation of points of view which can be described as black and white. It's interesting to note that the Bible often uses red as its describer for sin, as in Isaiah 1.18:

'Come now, let's settle this,' says the LORD. 'Though your sins are like scarlet, I will make them as white as snow. Though they are red like crimson, I will make them as white as wool.' (NLT)

If I was running this event again I would like to use red and white paint, which would give an added dimension as we think of the blood of Christ and his sacrifice on the cross. Perhaps that wouldn't fit so well with Halloween and the emphasis on darkness but it would avoid associating black with wrongdoing.

This leads us to the story of 'The Bonfire in the Darkness' as another way to give Christian meaning to the celebration of Halloween. For this we went back to the beach on what turned out to be a very dark and stormy night. The wind and rain whistled around us as we huddled close to one of the beach huts, which only had one door open so that there was some shelter from the elements if you went inside. Outside the hut we managed to light (and keep alight) a brazier, giving a source of both light and heat that was very welcome, given the weather.

The hut was to be used as a confessional booth and participants were invited to enter the hut, where they would find sheets of black card and some white pencils. On these they could write their deepest darkest secrets and the things that they were ashamed of and felt guilty about. These were not to be revealed to anyone, but to be kept by the writer for use later on. Once everyone had taken a turn in the confession hut and written about their sins, we lit a series of torches from the burning brazier and processed from the hut to the side of the lagoon about 100 metres away. Walking in the wind and rain made it incredibly hard to keep the torches alight, a metaphor perhaps for the difficulties we often face in keeping our eyes fixed on the light of God and the way our small flames of faith are so easily blown out by the chaos of life.

On reaching the lagoon I produced a small cardboard boat that one of our team had beautifully crafted, and invited everyone to place their scrumpled-up ball of confession paper into it. I'd prepped the floor of the boat with a little flame jelly, which is normally used for garden torches, and by huddling together to shelter the boat as much as possible from the wind, we managed to set it alight with one of the few torches that had survived from our procession.

Then the flaming boat was launched out into the lagoon, taking our confessions and all our darkest secrets away, in the manner of a Viking funeral. We watched the fragile little ship float into the middle of the lagoon, pushed there by the stormy wind, and marvelled as our darkest secrets created light and beauty in the midst of turmoil.

This was followed by a trek back to the hut, where everyone was given a white stone on which to write their name before we trudged down as close to the crashing waves as we dare and hurled these into the sea as an act of ritual washing, a form of baptism in the surf.

Returning to the beach hut, very damp and cold, we were heartened to find that the bonfire in the brazier had been turned into a barbecue and used to warm up hot dogs; the fire which had removed our sins had now become a source of sustenance for our new life, both physically and spiritually.

The experience of struggling with the wind and rain on the beach led us to move our Halloween events indoors to St Luke's

Prestonville, where I am the parish priest. We began with an event entitled 'Hallowed Light', the first in a series on the 'I Am' sayings of Jesus. The obvious one to focus on for Halloween was 'I am the light of the world', which we paired with the beginning of the Lord's prayer and the phrase 'hallowed be your name', as the festival is called All Hallows Eve. We emphasized the use of 'name' in this prayer and its relationship to identity.

We reflected on our own names and what those might mean, and what our relationship was to our own name – did we like it, loathe it, shorten it or have to explain it to people? Then we looked at the names of God in the Bible and in particular that name that God gave to Moses at the burning bush that we usually write as Yahweh and which means 'I Am'. Together we discovered, through some writings of Richard Rohr, that this name pronounced in Hebrew is thought by some to replicate the sound of breathing, especially as it is usually said under the speaker's breath in obedience to God's instruction that it should be unspoken. The revelation that comes from this understanding is that God is as close to us as our very breath, present with us from the moment of birth right through to our last breath.

While we thought about these concepts, we were all able to create a symbolic burning bush by slowly adding candles of various sizes to a central display stand while listening to a piece of music about light. This led us to move to thinking about who Jesus said that he was, and his assertion that he was the light of the world. Various Bible verses expressing this were read out:

John 8.12 Then Jesus spoke out, 'I am the light of the world. The one who follows me will never walk in darkness, but will have the light of life.' (NET)

1 John 1.5 This is the message we heard from Jesus and now declare to you: God is light, and there is no darkness in him at all. (NLT)

1 Thessalonians 5.5 For you are all children of the light and of the day; we don't belong to darkness and night. (NLT)

The Bible quotes ended with a few words from Julian of Norwich reflecting on this theme: 'Thus I saw and understood that our faith is our light in the night; which light is God, our endless day.'

In the course of creating these various Halloween events I realized we'd moved away from doing events in public spaces and gravitated towards coming back into church because that was the convenient thing to do. While this meant we were immune to the vagaries of the weather, it also meant that the event was less than fully public, in theory open to all, but actually only likely to be attended by those already in the know. My passion was to engage with the hordes of families who were out every Halloween night trick or treating and the partygoers preparing for a night on the town in their ghoulish costumes and make-up, so I invented the Hot Choc Stop.

I didn't want us to simply replicate what would be going on at the door of numerous houses in the area by giving out sweets, but to provide an alternative that would be valued by adults and children alike and give us a chance to talk about the true meaning of All Hallows Eve. There were two elements to this:

- Hot chocolate. The clue is in the title! I figured that people out on a dark evening on 31 October in the cold and quite probably wet might welcome the chance to stop for a few moments for a warming cup of hot chocolate with all the trimmings, including mini-marshmallows and whipped cream. This was easy to set up and not very expensive: a hot water urn in the church porch, a big tin of instant hot chocolate from the cash and carry along with a bucket of marshmallows and some recyclable paper cups.
- All Hallows Eve cards. These were modelled on the Top Trump format, like playing cards with a standard back that had an explanation of the true meaning of All Hallows Eve and a dozen or so different fronts featuring some unusual stories of saints. The idea was to give these out to children and encourage them to see if they could collect a set by swapping with their friends or coming to the Hot Choc Stop again.

The back of the cards explained All Hallows Eve as follows:

There is a festival that is celebrated on 31 October every year – do you know what it is? You might know it as 'Halloween' but did you know that Halloween actually takes its name from a church festival? All Hallows Day happens on 1 November and it is the time that Christians remember 'all those who are holy'. These people are often called 'saints' (you can read about one on the other side of this card) and they lived, followed and sometimes died for their faith in Jesus, and they are who we celebrate on 'All Hallows'.

We tried to make the cards fun with amusing cartoons of the featured saints and by picking out some of the more unusual saint stories, like St Cassian of Imola, a fourth-century schoolmaster and Christian who refused to offer sacrifice to the pagan gods and was stabbed to death by his students with their pencils! Or St Clement, who was Pope from AD 88 to 99 and who was martyred by being tied to an anchor and thrown into the sea.

There are many saint stories like these and children are fascinated by them, and they offer a little light relief to an evening
which can be a bit scary for those who are afraid of ghosts and
ghouls.

To join in the fun, I also encourage our volunteers to dress
up in some sort of saint costume. One of the helpers managed
to create a roman toga from an old sheet and studded it with
broken pencils and streaks of 'blood' as a tribute to St Cassian. I
have dressed up as Martin Luther, as 31 October is his feast day,
but no one ever recognizes that and just thinks I'm a priest who
dresses a little weirdly!

Typically, 400 or so people stop by for a drink, a chat and to
be given some cards, and there are lots of opportunities to have
open conversations about the meaning of All Hallows Eve and
what a saint is. Most of those who stop are families but there is
always a smattering of adults on their way out to the pub or a
bar ready for a party night in their Halloween costumes. More
importantly, it's great PR for the church on a night that many
churches actively avoid because they see it as evil.

I think sometimes the church is too timid when it comes to
engaging with elements in society that can be seen as spiritualist
or pagan. There is no doubt we need to be careful with the occult
and the whole world of ghosts, spiritualism and what might be
termed mystic tradition, but these themes do connect for some
people and there is an opportunity to link this to Christianity for
those who are bold enough. Initiatives such as the Jesus deck and
Ruach cards are examples of products created by people who
have taken the tarot card format and given it a more explicitly
Christian twist. The Bible doesn't shy away from these themes,
and devils feature at least 35 times in the New Testament. If the
writers of scripture didn't shy away from it then neither should
we.

Part of what it means to go outside of church in our exploration of mission is to go outside the accepted norms of church
practice because it's often in the margins of acceptability that
we can find the spirit and have an opportunity for theologically
rich and complex discussions. This requires some courage and a

certain robustness of faith that is not easy or right for everyone, so requires careful consideration before we embark on projects like this.

Things to consider

- Understand your own spiritual limits and don't stretch your theology beyond what you think you can cope with.
- Be prepared to discuss risky ideas with others in an open and honest way.
- Consider how you might do something distinctively different from everyone else on an evening such as Halloween.
- Are there other 'forbidden' folk traditions that can be explored as an opportunity for epiphany?
- Pay attention to health and safety when serving hot drinks – not too hot for children and be careful about allergies and special dietary requirements.

9

Theatrical Spirituality

It's not always practical to run events in the open air given the vagaries of the UK weather and climate change. One of the reasons we stopped doing the Beach Hut Advent Calendar after 2018 was because being on the beach at 6 p.m. every December for 11 years I noticed that the weather had got considerably more rainy and windy, which is consistent with the prediction that climate change will make UK winters warmer and wetter. Beyond began life in a different kind of public space from a church as we rented a studio theatre for all our events for the first year. This is clearly less public than being outdoors but theatres appeal to a different kind of audience than a church building, and as we were aiming our work at a cultural demographic that is interested in art this seemed like a reasonable way to start. The important thing was to ensure good publicity outside the usual church circles so that the work could reach a wider, more diverse crowd.

For the very first event it made sense to focus on visual art as a way of seeing God, and the evening was titled 'Seeing is Believing'. A few months beforehand I had been to an art exhibition that featured a number of guerrilla artists including some graffiti work. One of the artists styled himself My Dog Sighs and he was part of a group of artists who took part in Free Art Fridays. They would send each other artwork in the post and on Fridays they would each go out and leave the art in public places for people to discover and take home. My Dog Sighs' own speciality was little painted figures on A4-sized scraps of cardboard posed in a crucifixion stance and sometimes including the words 'Am I Your God?' somewhere in the frame. The piece I had seen at the exhibition was called 'crucifiction' and was one of the first artworks I had ever bought.

His work fascinated me and I contacted him to ask if he would be prepared to come and take part in the Seeing is Believing event doing some live painting. He also was intrigued, and although he wouldn't describe himself as Christian, he acknowledged that there was something that drew him to the crucifixion in his art practice so he agreed to come, and the plan was hatched for him to paint live during the evening.

We needed to create more content for the evening than just having someone painting, and as a team we began to discuss how we saw God and what kind of imagery helped us with this. We talked about nature, we talked about Jesus, we talked about seeing God in others, we talked about discovering God through being creative. Three themes began to emerge in our discussions: God in nature, God through the person of Jesus, God in the image of created human beings. This became the structure for our event, a three-act story of images of God through presentation, interaction and creative activity.

One of the advantages of using a theatre is that it automatically has a dramatic essence and there is a sense of anticipation when you enter the space, which in this case was surrounded by black curtains, set with some small tables and chairs arranged in groups, with a slightly raised staging area on one side of the theatre. Spotlights focused on various parts of the space, highlighting a wall of beautiful nature photographs, a small, rugged driftwood cross and the artist already at work on the stage with paint and canvases. A projector and screen were set up in one corner, a constant presence at all our indoor events and a key part of every evening. The message on the screen from the beginning encouraged attendees to explore the various activities ranged around the room. After ten minutes I gave a short welcome and introduction to the evening, and focused everyone's attention on My Dog Sighs, who had already completed two canvases as he had set himself the target of painting one every five minutes throughout the event. Once a canvas was finished, he propped it up at the front of the stage for everyone to see.

Then the lights were dimmed and the distinctive tones of the late Sir John Gielgud boomed around the dark theatre, unique in its diction and intonation despite the hiss and crackle from the old recording, and we heard the familiar words from the beginning of the Bible announcing the formation of everything: 'In the beginning God created the heaven and the earth.'

As we listened, we could also watch images of stars in the sky, fish in the sea, birds in the air, beasts on the plains, all moving in majestic beauty as those sonorous tones recounted the ancient story of creation.

Within the confines of this studio performance space, we were reminded of the wonder of creation and invited to attribute this wonder to God, in the same way that the writer of Romans was trying to express himself when he wrote, 'Ever since the world was created, people have seen the earth and sky. Through everything God made, they can clearly see his invisible qualities – his eternal power and divine nature' (Romans 1.20, NLT).

Ironically, we couldn't see the earth or sky because we were indoors with no immediate access to the natural world we were asking people to focus on. We were attempting to remind people of the wonder of nature while the real thing in the form of a beach, a blue sky and a gloriously sunny day was only 100 yards away from the door of our chosen venue. Our artificial version of nature was made up of images of natural wonder shown on the screen, in harmony with the nature exhibition arranged along one of the black curtained walls. Many people find their connection to God through nature and this first act was a chance to focus on this.

We took the transition between the chapters of our event as a kind of intermission and a chance to revisit the artist and see where he'd got to with his work, before moving to a section about human beings. The lighting changed and some curtains were pulled back to reveal an expanse of white wall with a number of A3 sheets of paper attached to it. Spotlights had been arranged so that people standing in front of the paper cast shadows and we had two volunteers with pens who were on hand to trace a silhouette of each individual, creating a personal portrait that was then handed to them to keep. In another part of the room was a laptop set up with a camera showing a distorted image of whoever stood in front of it.

I introduced the idea that we are all made in the image of God and again that recording of John Gielgud continued the reading from Genesis 1: God created man in his own image, in the image of God created he him; male and female created he them. (Genesis 1.35 KJV)

Everyone was invited to either explore the silhouette activity or to partner up with another person on their table and attempt to make a quick sketch of the other without looking down at the paper they were drawing on or removing their pencil from the paper. This activity was drawn to a close after 15 minutes by asking everyone to collect two different-coloured sticky notes and write on the green one an attribute about themselves which is divine and on the red one something that they think is not God-like.

This took us to the next intermission and the chance to check in with My Dog Sighs, who by now had completed eight canvases and was busily engaged in creating number nine. The lighting changed once more to highlight a series of alcoves that framed the entrance to the theatre where there was a display of very varied images of Jesus from the series 'The Christ We Share' by CMS. This features paintings of Jesus from around the world showing how different cultures have a diverse view of him from the white, bearded hippy that we so often think of in the West. Introducing this section with words from Colossians 1.15 – 'Jesus is the visible image of the invisible God' (NLT) – I then played a video I had edited using a whole variety of images and clips of Jesus that I had collected from films, videos and stills.

We asked everyone to chat on their tables about their image of Jesus, trying to avoid the 'gentle Jesus meek and mild' approach as much as possible. Everyone was also invited to view the images on display in the alcoves and to write their feelings about them on sticky notes and fix these to the walls beside the pictures. These responses were so varied and included 'outspoken', 'generous', 'trustworthy', 'a listener' and 'judgemental'. For me this started the principle of allowing people to respond in the way they see fit without any judgement or comment, which has informed all of the work of Beyond.

This was the final act of our three-part story, and the journey from considering the image of God we see in nature, in each other and through Jesus was a very rich way of exploring this theme. Throughout the evening, My Dog Sighs had diligently worked away at his paintings, completing one every five minutes so that he could keep to his self-imposed schedule of 12 canvases within the 60-minutes of the event. Eventually he ended up with a dozen little plaintive characters, each looking out at us and asking, 'Am I Your God?'

I handed over to him as the event drew to a close and he invited people to come forward and stand beside the painting that they identified with the most. As they gravitated towards their favourite images, he encouraged individuals to pick them up so that everyone could see the image more clearly. He then announced that the bearer of each portrait could keep it as a gift from him. A moment of gratitude erupted into the studio as he made this generous gesture. The small canvases held in the arms of a dozen people became holy relics of an evening spent examining our image of God, to be taken home and treasured as a reminder of the moment when an artist broke down the boundary between earth and heaven with the simple donation of his talent and an act of beauty.

Later, online, My Dog Sighs found himself reflecting profoundly on this 'church' experience. He wrote on his blog:

> I really struggled with this brief.
> - my view of God.
> - one hour to paint in.
> - in front of a live audience.
> I hoped that the audience might be drawn to one specific painting, identifying some aspect as something they associate with their own idea of 'god'.

The blog turned into an online discussion as text dropped into the comment box about the nature of faith and personal experiences of art and spirituality appeared from cyberspace. One of the commenters asked if this had affected his view of God at all. My Dog Sighs replied:

> I suppose everything I do affects my view of god. It's just the term god and how it's shared and creates a view of god we must follow. God as a person/father niggles with me. God as everything I suppose I can get my head around. Every atom, every event. But then we are all god and I'm not sure the church would like that.

We talk in the Christian world about a personal God and having a personal relationship with God and yet we expect faithful followers to adhere to a codified template laid down by the church. We present an objective set of dogmas and beliefs about God for people to 'sign up to' which don't seem to allow for subjective interpretation or discovery. We bind ourselves to words and statements of faith and creeds and conditions, forgetting that we are all unique and respond to God in our own unique way. Isn't this what personal faith means? Shouldn't we be cultivating as many different views of God as we can in some sort of attempt to explore what we mean when we describe God as infinite?

That's why art is so important as a way to discover more about God because art is always subjective and personal. We each respond to a piece of art in our own unique way, just as we respond to God in our own unique way. And, by the way, it doesn't need to be 'religious' art, in fact sometimes that can be a hindrance. Learning to see God in the intensity of a colour; in the complexity of an idea; in the cleverness of concept; in the expertise of the craft – these are all ways to God that go beyond the printed or spoken word which so much of church is wedded to. The ingenuity of human creativity should continually point us to the source of that creativity in the one who made heaven and earth.

The people who came along all responded in their own personal way:

'My understanding of how God resonates in the world was affirmed.'
'Good to have time to explore ideas/feelings with others in a safe environment.'
'Reminded me of how amazing God is!'
'It inspired me to be more creative.'
'Helped me clarify my thoughts on Jesus – what type of human he was.'

This was an opportunity to have our own experience of seeing and believing in the God who speaks to us in so many different ways.

How else could we use our theatre bookings to help people explore their understanding of God? What about a comedy night asking whether God has a sense of humour? Religion is so often seen as serious and boring with no opportunity for any kind of fun as that kind of thing is frowned upon. But God inhabits all of our emotions, including our propensity to laugh, and the Bible is full of humour if you just know where to look. Who is the greatest comedian in the Bible? Samson, because he brought the house down.

When God tells Abraham that his 90-year-old wife is going to have a baby, he literally falls on his face he finds it such a joke, and this is compounded when God tells them to name the child Isaac, which means laughter. The psalmist says: 'Our mouths were filled with laughter' (Psalm 126.2, NIV); even the writer of Ecclesiastes, who is generally so full of gloom about the plight of human beings, recommends that we should have some fun! We thought it would be good to investigate if G. K. Chesterton was right when he said: 'It is the test of a good religion whether you can joke about it.'

Some time ago I was a performer and one of the projects I got involved with was comedy improvisation with a group of other Christian performers. We were never very successful but one of our group went on to much greater fame and now tours the country doing comedy shows – Milton Jones. I knew Milton was interested in the interface between comedy and worship and so I booked him for our next event.

The Argus, Saturday, May 24 – Sunday, May 25, 2008

—————————— **NEWS** ——————————

Comic's light-hearted take on spirituality

IF YOU thought God was no laughing matter then think again.

Comedian Milton Jones will be helping people see spirituality in a different light at the Old Market Theatre, Hove, tomorrow.

The event is part of Beyond, a project funded by the Diocese of Chichester which explores non-traditional ways of being Christian.

Organiser and stipendiary minister the Rev Martin Poole said: "It is an attempt to get out of churches. We are

trying to find new ways of doing church which do not involve going to church. It mainly came about through a passion I have to communicate differently and the diocese was keen for me to come up with some ideas.

"I was originally an actor and now I'm a television producer so I have always been interested in thinking creatively."

The Beyond project is part of nation-wide organisation Fresh Expressions which helps Church of England and

Methodist congregations develop new ways of worship. There are more than 500 projects across the country.

Mr Poole said: "We have three specific target groups. The first is experienced church people who are used to going to a parish church but are perhaps interested in thinking about about their faith in a different way.

"The second group are what we call dechurched – 30% of the population used to be involved but are no longer. We are also aiming at people who are

interested in spirituality but do not think church is for them."

Being a stipendiary minister means Mr Poole has no parish of his own. He said: "I'm in a very privileged position. I do not have to keep a church building going or do all the other things ordinary parish priests get involved in."

Events are planned for the last Sunday of each month. Funny Spirituality is at The Old Market tomorrow at 7pm. For more details, visit www.beyond-church.co.uk.

We didn't want the evening to be a simple stand-up night. You can get that in any comedy club and they would do a much funnier job than a group of arty religious types doing this for the first time. 'Joy is the most infallible sign of the presence of God', wrote Léon Bloy, and we wanted our evening to explore how humour can reveal truths about God that go much deeper than ordinary talk. Our friend Andrew Rumsey wrote on the Ship of Fools website:

Comedy lies in the gaps between what we ought to be, what we are, and what we just might be one day. Comic timing relies on eternity being written into the heart of man, and man knowing the absurd shortfall: bathos – the lapse from sublime to ridiculous – is thus a part of the comedian's stock-in-trade. In the biblical story, though, God appears to fool around with this familiar routine in the person of Jesus, whose resurrection rewrites the joke about the bloke who's alive, but then dies. The timing seems to be all over the place, but, for those who get it (and Christianity is a gag that plenty don't), the divine punchline makes sense of everything that went before.

Our evening began with the theatre set out like a comedy club with a large projector screen and a solo mic. The screen showed a rolling selection of slides of jokey church noticeboards. After a short introduction I set the scene by showing two video clips, one of Eddie Izzard talking about how dreary church hymns usually are, and a sketch from a Monty Python stage show with an academic giving a lecture about different types of joke which was simultaneously being illustrated by three straight-faced, boiler-suited demonstrators using bananas, planks and custard pies.

Comedy should include some audience participation so on each table was a collection of Christmas-cracker jokes and we opened the floor to anyone who wanted to read out any of these while one of our team ran around with a radio mic. Then came the science bit, as they used to say in the commercials, a series of facts and figures about humour such as that there are three types of laughter: incongruity/unexpectedness, superiority which is usually misfortune-based, and relief when tension is broken. The average person laughs 17 times per day; laughter strengthens human connections, laughter uses the whole brain and laughter has health benefits.

This led us on to consider laughter clubs with a US news report about a phenomenon that had developed in India of a club where people could go for half an hour of laughing before they went to work. It included an interview with a 'joyologist' talking about the health benefits of laughter and how people are using laughter therapy to help those with mental health issues and even those with multiple sclerosis. At first I thought this was an April Fool news item but it turns out to be true!

Having done some study of laughter and given it some biblical context it was time to turn the evening over to Milton. He took us on a journey from a straightforward stand-up comedy routine with jokes like 'Why is Christianity like a Cornish pasty – we all know there's something in it but it's difficult to find out exactly what it is', through some reflections about the use of the words 'Christ' and 'Jesus' as swear words and words of holiness to eventual contemplation on the meaning of life and the place of faith in that.

It was inspiring to sit for half an hour and be taken from hilarious comedy to a place of spiritual depth by such a professional, and by the end of the evening there was a reverential hush in the theatre and a real feeling that God was present. Afterwards people said: 'I learnt that relaxation is Godly'; 'We should see more fun in our God-given life'; 'I learnt something new about God, myself and others.' It turned out God did have a sense of humour and that maybe whoever said 'God is a comedian playing to an audience too afraid to laugh' was right.

You don't need to be personal friends with a stand-up comedian to be able to host a night about religion and humour: there are plenty of Christian comedians who can be booked for an evening, there are even some vicars who do stand-up in their spare time, and you might even have some comedy talent of your own which you could try out.

After having a good laugh, we thought it would be appropriate to have some good clean fun, so our next theatre event was called 'Clean', and it began with some dirt. On the floor of the entrance to the theatre we taped a large white cloth that people had to walk over in order to get in. Typically, for once it was a lovely, dry sunny day outside so we had to mix up some mud and scatter it around outside the theatre for people to step in before they entered, otherwise the cloth would have stayed as white as the driven snow. Later on, that cloth became the centrepiece for our evening, which was shaped around the idea of one long confession. In a regular church service confession comes at the beginning and often we skate over it quite quickly, but this event was an opportunity to really think about how we have spoiled things or been spoiled, and to actively do something about that.

On entering the theatre people found one of our volunteers sitting at a table with a tub of soapy water and a washboard, scrubbing away at some dirty cloths; this continued throughout the whole evening. The usual scattering of tables and chairs was arranged around a large central table holding a paddling pool with a little battery-operated fountain, recycling the water and making a gentle trickling sound.

Once everyone was settled and seated, we showed a short clip from the opening ceremony of the 2008 Beijing Olympics where the teams of athletes walked over a large multicoloured ink pad before stepping on a white platform, so that gradually as more and more athletes made that journey the white platform became a rainbow made from their coloured footprints. This was the precursor to our bringing in the white cloth that everyone had tramped muddy footprints onto and hanging it in a prominent position in the theatre as an icon of grime.

This led into a short presentation about the relationship between cleanliness and religion. We were reminded that the Israelite story centres around salvation through water, and to bring that home we watched Charlton Heston driving back the waters of the Red Sea from the epic film *The Ten Commandments*. We learnt a little about Mikvah, the Jewish rite of ritual washing, and that the Romans prized cleanliness so much that they would often spend as long as two hours every day bathing.

In contrast to this, Christianity in the Middle Ages seemed to take great pride in being dirty. Abandoning Jewish and Roman practice, early Christians viewed bathing as a form of hedonism; they embraced saints like Godric, who, to mortify the flesh, walked from England to Jerusalem without washing or changing his clothes. St Jerome is quoted as saying: 'He who has bathed in Christ has no need of a second bath', and the Arabic epic *One Thousand and One Nights* has this to say about Christians: 'Christians never wash, for, at their birth, ugly men in black garments pour water over their heads, and this ablution, accompanied by strange gestures, frees them from all obligation of washing for the rest of their lives.'

This section concluded with the oft-quoted comment supposedly made by Queen Elizabeth I that she bathed 'once a year whether I need to or not'. This is an apocryphal quote which until recently was included in GCSE history books but has since been removed as it is untrue. Elizabeth I had some very sumptuous bathrooms built in her palaces and seemed to take great care of her hygiene until she was in her old age, and the quote is more likely to be a joke that was written around the beginning of the twentieth century.

This was contrasted with the fact that these days in the UK more than £10.5 billion is spent on beauty products every year: that's at least £2,000 per person. Then we moved to the science bit, just like a famous brand of beauty products used to say in their advertising. Scientists have tested what they call the 'Macbeth effect', after Lady Macbeth, who imagines that her hands are still soiled after murdering Duncan and cries, 'Out, damned spot! Out, I say!' We tried this scientific test for ourselves.

We invited everyone to take a few minutes to remember something unpleasant that they did in the past, then asked them to complete these words:

W _ _ H
SH _ _ ER
S _ _ P

Without fail everyone wrote; WASH, SHOWER, SOAP.

But these aren't the only words that use these letters and participants in the test who hadn't been asked to think of something unpleasant were just as likely to write WISH, SHAKER, STEP or some other words such as slap, slop, wilt, welt, shaper or shamer.

Picasso is said to have believed that: 'The purpose of art is washing the dust of daily life off our souls', and we got a chance to think about this and what we regard as wholesome or not by looking at a range of nice and nasty pictures placed around the walls and writing our reactions on them. At the same time these images were also being shown on the projector screen and for ten minutes the room was a quiet hush as we reflected on what we thought to be wholesome and what unclean.

Once everyone was seated again, we posed three questions:

'What do I need to forgive myself for?'
'What do I need to forgive others for?'
'What do I need to be forgiven for?'

White laminated cards and marker pens were then distributed for everyone to write with. We explained that this was to be done in total privacy; no one would read what was written on the sheet and no one would be asked to read out what they'd written. It's important when asking people to express confidential things about themselves that they know what will happen to their words because really honest confessions can only be made in private in a confirmed safe space. While people were doing this the screen showed an excerpt from the BBC transmission of *Manchester Passion*, when Keith Allen, playing the part of Pilate, washes his hands of Jesus and then goes on to explain the physical torture of crucifixion.

Confessions written, we then distributed wet wipes and everyone was invited to wipe their sheet clean. Then all the dirty cloths were collected up and taken to the muddy footprint-covered sheet where it was revealed that the middle of the sheet contained a cross made of white double-sided tape that still had its backing on. We removed this, revealing the sticky tape underneath and the soiled wet wipes were stuck to this, creating a breathtaking cross of raggedy cloth which became our focal point as we recited a visual confession liturgy with images on the projector screen.

The conclusion to the event featured one last short film, a TV commercial for Sony cameras showing a whole block of streets in Miami being flooded with millions of litres of party foam,

as sometimes used in nightclubs. As bubbles floated and flowed around on-screen, coating children and adults who were smiling and dancing in delight, we also started up a small bubble machine and began handing out little pots of bubble liquid to everyone and guiding them towards the paddling pool in the centre of the room to properly clean off their laminated sheets and to enjoy cleansing themselves in the water, filling the air with their own bubbles as we were now all clean.

We closed with words from Psalm 51 while we listened to a Kyrie song:

Psalm 51
Soak me in your laundry and I'll be clean,
scrub me and I'll have a snow-white life.
Tune me in to foot-tapping songs,
set these once-broken bones to dancing.

Don't look too close for blemishes,
give me a clean bill of health.
God, make a fresh start in me,
shape a Genesis week from the chaos of my life.
Don't throw me out with the trash,
or fail to breathe holiness in me.
Bring me back from gray exile, put a fresh wind in my sails!
Give me a job teaching rebels your ways
so the lost can find their way home.
Commute my death sentence, God, my salvation God,
and I'll sing anthems to your life-giving ways.
Unbutton my lips, dear God; I'll let loose with your praise.
Psalm 51.7–15 (*The Message*)

As a final keepsake to remind all attendees that they are cleansed
and forgiven, everyone was given a small bar of soap to take home.

Stillness is important to many people of faith and there is a
long history of silent reflection and prayer as part of church
tradition, from monastic contemplation and retreats through to
prayer spaces in city-centre churches and side chapels in cathedrals set aside for silent prayer. Theatres are generally places of
hush and quiet concentration although in recent years the intru-
sion of mobile phones has sometimes disturbed that peace, so we
thought we'd examine stillness and silence in the theatre that we
were using for our monthly events.

'Still' began with some frenetic activities designed to hype us
all up and replicate a sense of the stress of daily life experienced
by so many. We watched the 1950s film *London to Brighton in
Four Minutes*, a speeded-up version of the train journey which
was relevant to us as we are in Brighton. This was followed up
by a short explanation from one of our team who was a professional counsellor about stress and the harm that does to us.

To help people experience some stress, we asked everyone to
play the chocolate party game. In the centre of the space was a
table with no chairs and a large bar of chocolate, plate, knife and
fork and some hats and gloves. Each table around the room had
a couple of dice and these were thrown until someone rolled a

double six, then that person had to rush out to the table, don a hat and gloves and try to eat some chocolate with the knife and fork while other tables continued to roll their dice to get their chance to eat chocolate. It's a fast game with everyone shouting encouragement to their table mates as they rushed to eat as much chocolate as possible before they were shoved aside by someone else. After two or three minutes playing the game, I called a halt and asked everyone to sit in silence and stillness for two minutes before continuing the competition. We did this a few times to emphasize the difference between racing around and stillness.

Eventually the game was stopped and we invited everyone to sit quietly for a time of meditation, to close their eyes and listen to some gentle music as we guided them through a short time of reflection. It began with the usual sorts of phrases – 'Focus on your breathing', 'Become aware of your posture', 'Listen to the sounds around you', 'Empty your mind' – but gradually introduced more and more unsettling thoughts: 'Did you lock the car?', 'Are you going to lose your job soon?', 'How do you feel about your mother?' We wanted to show that even in stillness and quiet, our minds can take us to stressful places that cause internal turmoil; simply being quiet isn't always a solution to our stress. Being still is an emotional, psychological and physical state and the path to know God truly is best found when we are able to be still in all these aspects of our personality.

After listening to a version of 'Be Still and Know that I am God' we heard a short Bible reading:

> As evening came, Jesus said to his disciples, 'Let's cross to the other side of the lake.' So they took Jesus in the boat and started out, leaving the crowds behind. But soon a fierce storm came up. High waves were breaking into the boat, and it began to fill with water. Jesus was sleeping at the back of the boat with his head on a cushion. The disciples woke him up, shouting, 'Teacher, don't you care that we're going to drown?' When Jesus woke up, he rebuked the wind and said to the waves, 'Silence! Be still!' Suddenly the wind stopped, and there was a great calm. Mark 4.35–39 (NLT)

This led into a five-minute silent meditation with words animating on the screen but no audio of any kind:

How often are you still?
Try this
Slowly
Make yourself comfortable
Begin breathing slowly as you read
Notice breathing in
Notice breathing out
Feel your ribs move with every breath
Notice all your senses
What can you see?
What can you hear?
What can you smell?
What can you taste?
What are you touching?
Focus on where you are now
Be now
Be here
Be still
Be still and know that I am God
Know that I am God, always

Being still and silent with a group of people, especially when the intention is to pray or focus on God, is a tremendously powerful experience. People who are on a path to recovery from addictions of one kind or another often go through the 12-step process and a step-11 group usually features 20 minutes of silence in a group setting and is one of the most spiritual activities that takes place in the church that I serve. I am not a great fan of silent retreats myself but many people find them extremely helpful as part of their spiritual practice, and this event was intended to help people understand a little of why that might be, along with a taster of intentional spiritual silence with the hope that it might encourage attendees to seek out more ways to be still in their own faith journey.

Things to consider

- Think about using a space that is usually frequented by non-church folk and make your event attractive to them and publicize it to them.
- Use any contacts you may have to find artists who would be interested in collaborating on an event.
- Create a narrative structure to your event so that it has a beginning, middle and end.
- Read around the topic you've chosen for the event so as to be able to represent a range of voices and opinions.
- Make full use of the facilities a theatre provides as part of the hire, including tech support if it's available.
- Theatre spaces provoke a sense of drama; use this to enhance your event.
- Find ways to help people engage with each other in a non-threatening way.
- Remember: all art can reflect something of our creator God.

Pub Theology

I love chatting in pubs, lots of people do, and lots of people have quite philosophical discussions in pubs although that can frequently depend on how much they've had to drink! A pub is not quite a fully open public space in the way that a park, street or seafront is, but it's still more comfortable, and certainly more common, for many people to enter a pub than it is a church. When choosing to use a pub as a venue it must also be recognized that this is not necessarily a comfortable place for everyone, especially those who are in some form of recovery.

After a full year of running monthly events in a studio theatre at some considerable expense, we decided to try another type of venue and moved Beyond into a pub. This had the advantage of being a lot cheaper and had a much more informal atmosphere, the disadvantage being that we didn't have the facilities of a theatre and had to adapt the venue each time we used it. Ironically this gave us much more freedom, and the conviviality of sitting round tables with a drink changes the ambience of any event considerably and is much better for encouraging discussion.

All of the events described in this chapter took place in a pub function room but with a few adaptations they could just as easily be set in a community hall, large living room or even a church hall. Pub function rooms each have their own character, often featuring mirrors or old Victorian etched glass, and at the very least there are likely to be stacks of glasses, glinting and sparkling in the light. So 'Reflections' became the theme we thought we would explore in the particular pub function room that had been kind enough to allow us in once a month.

In our initial ideas session we decided we wanted the evening to take people on a journey from examining how we see ourselves, through a process of self-realization and reflection to look at how we see God. The word reflection has a double meaning as obviously it refers to mirrors and the process of seeing, but is also about meditative analysis and contemplation. There are lots of themes to think about between these two meanings and we wanted the evening to explore all aspects of this through four phases of exploration:

- How we see ourselves
- How others see us
- How God sees us
- How we see God/how we reflect God (realizing that our understanding or reflecting about the image of God is often distorted due to our own experience).

We set the room up with various mirrors, some made from distorted mirrored Perspex while others were just squares of plane mirror scattered around the room. There were two reflective installations, including a mock dressing table which only held fragments of mirror in its frame and a projection screen with a hole cut in it which was placed in front of a mirror.

As everyone came in, they were given a small shard of mirror and asked to find a table to sit at with their drinks. A woman came in and sat in front of the dressing table brushing her hair and trying to see herself in the shards while we watched a short film: people entering a washroom found themselves facing a mirror of truth that revealed words written on their foreheads outlining which of the seven deadly sins they had committed. Everyone was then invited to move around the room to experience the different reflective installations. At this point the projection screen with the hole began showing different images of people with their face removed so that participants could put their head into the hole and see themselves reflected in the mirror as Gandhi or the Queen or Madonna or even Jesus on the cross.

Everyone was asked to sit after ten minutes and stare at themselves in one of the squares of ordinary mirror for five minutes.

This is a technique called mirror gazing and is an intentional form of meditation which can be quite uncomfortable, as most people don't often spend that long looking at themselves with no other purpose. While this was going on we listened to 'Man in the Mirror' by Michael Jackson, someone who had a very conflicted attitude to his own image.

Pens were then handed out and everyone was asked to see if they could trace an image of themselves on their mirror and write a few words about what they would like to change about themselves. Copies of a number of different articles from *The Guardian*'s series 'What I see in the mirror' were handed out for people to read, as these often give interesting insight into the kinds of things that celebrities like or hate about themselves. This activity was drawn together by one of the volunteers reading from Corinthians:

> Now we see things imperfectly, like puzzling reflections in a mirror, but then we will see everything with perfect clarity. All that I know now is partial and incomplete, but then I will know everything completely, just as God now knows me completely. 1 Corinthians 13.12 (NLT)

This was followed by a time for discussion about what we think this might mean.

Finally, we had another short reading from Corinthians, reminding us that we have a role to play in reflecting divine values to the rest of the world:

> So all of us who have had that veil removed can see and reflect the glory of the Lord. And the Lord – who is the Spirit – makes us more and more like him as we are changed into his glorious image. 2 Corinthians 3.18 (NLT)

The evening concluded with a short clip from one of the Harry Potter films about the Mirror of Erised, a mirror that shows you what you really desire (as the word ERISED is DESIRE reflected). As everyone left, they were given a small black card with a shard of mirror glued onto it and the words: 'Right now I glimpse the truth, but one day I will know everything, just as God knows me.'

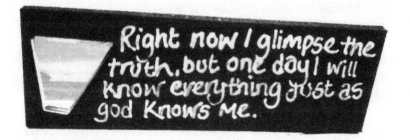

The challenge we set ourselves for the next event was all about helping people to consider a different perspective on their lives and to look forward to the year ahead. We specifically wanted to consider God's three-dimensional view of time/life as a way of keeping ourselves from over-focusing on the miniscule details of living, and to give people the opportunity to consider the 'big picture' as if viewing life from a mountain-top, looking at and assimilating their past, present and future and creating an opportunity to stop, think and appreciate. We titled this evening 'Vistas' and viewed it very much as a discussion starter. One of the advantages of being in a pub was the opportunity for further discussion and we realized that we often fill the hour of the event with content and that people might like a chance to reflect and discuss more at length, so we proposed to meet in the main pub bar again two weeks later just to discuss 'Vistas', having had some time to let the ideas and themes of that night percolate in our minds.

A vista is described in the dictionary as 'a view, especially a beautiful view from a high position', something of a challenge to create in the dingy upper room of an old pub! In preparation for this I went out with a camera to a variety of locations and took a succession of photos while turning around 360 degrees (this was before the advent of a panoramic setting on smartphones which would make this a lot easier now!). I then printed these photos and collaged them together to form a long strip photo. As a team we chose a panorama of the Brighton seafront, complete with beach huts, the promenade, seagulls and the sea, and I stuck these together to form a giant hoop with all the photos on the inside. Our preparation for the event involved suspending this from the ceiling so that it was level at head height. To give people a sense of scale and as an introduction to the theme of vistas they were invited to duck inside the hoop when they arrived and experience a virtual view of the seafront in a full 360 degree immersive visual.

Other activities as people came in were to view various landscape images and some regular flat panoramic photographs that were on display in a large format showing lots of detail. When people went to the bar to get a drink, they were first asked to measure out a piece of ribbon equivalent to their age using a scale which was stuck to the bar surface and to keep this piece of ribbon with them throughout the evening.

Once everyone had a drink and was settled, we introduced the idea of different ways of seeing. This began with a timelapse video of some artists creating a chalk drawing on a seafront promenade which was an optical illusion of a large canyon. Viewed from a certain angle it was realistic enough to make you think that the tarmac gave way to an enormous chasm but you only had to move a few feet to left or right to realize the deception. We also showed various other examples of street art that rely on our perception of three-dimensional space to fool us into thinking that the pavements on which the art is drawn are full of holes or water or even have objects sticking out of them that might obstruct us.

We then viewed a short video clip of Rob Bell talking about time and how we only have a one-dimensional view of time, but that God has a three-dimensional view of time and has no constraints on how to view time. This we illustrated with some Bible verses from the New Living Translation:

The LORD looks down from heaven and sees the whole human race. From his throne he observes all who live on the earth. He made their hearts, so he understands everything they do. (Psalm 33.13–15)

God alone understands the way to wisdom; he knows where it can be found, for he looks throughout the whole earth and sees everything under the heavens. (Job 28.23–24)

'My thoughts are nothing like your thoughts,' says the LORD. And my ways are far beyond anything you could imagine. For just as the heavens are higher than the earth, so my ways are higher than your ways and my thoughts higher than your thoughts.' (Isaiah 55.8–9)

As an illustration of how human perspectives can change, we watched and listened to the voices of the crew of Apollo 8 reading from Genesis 1 as they filmed the earth rising above the surface of the moon during their first orbit around it, and a quote from one of the Shuttle astronauts:

For those who have seen the Earth from space, and for the hundreds and perhaps thousands more who will, the experience most certainly changes your perspective.

The things that we share in our world are far more valuable than those which divide us. (Donald Williams, Shuttle astronaut)

To encourage discussion, we handed round sheets with quotes about perspective from various famous folk such as C. S. Lewis, Albert Einstein and Salman Rushdie, and allowed the conversations to flow for ten minutes. This time of open discussion closed with an introduction to the idea of thin places. This comes from a Celtic saying that heaven and earth are only three feet apart, but in some places that distance is even smaller. A thin place is where the veil that separates heaven and earth is lifted and one is able to receive a glimpse of the glory of God as the perceiver senses the existence of a world beyond what we know through our five senses alone. To illustrate this sense of a different perspective we were able to play some audio of a short talk by Dave Tomlinson about this concept.

We were all then directed back to the lengths of ribbon which we had acquired at the beginning of the event and asked to write on it our favourite thin places, either particular geographic locations or 'spiritual' places such as 'with my children' or 'walking the dog'. Contributions included walking in the country, moonbathing and even the Tube! Everyone was then invited to attach their ribbon to the arms of a cross that had been set up in one corner of the bar as both an illustration of spiritual places special to us and of the variety of years represented by the range of ages in the room. A perspective on both time and place.

Finally, we considered Jesus' transfiguration, which gave the disciples who accompanied him to that mountaintop a very different perspective on their leader and teacher. A continuation of the audio talk by Dave Tomlinson encouraged us to seek out the everyday gleams of glory that give us a glimpse of God: the laughter of a child, a pint of cool beer on a summer's day or the feel of standing on sand in bare feet. These ordinary everyday experiences can change our perspective so that we're aware of the vast vista of the divine all around us.

As an extended conclusion to this vista theme, we invited everyone to join us in a trip up to Devil's Dyke on the South Downs, just a 20-minute drive from the pub, so that we could marvel at an enormous night-time vista of stars and sky, city and sea. The evening was crystal clear and dry and on the downs we were greeted by a truly awe-inspiring view of the Milky Way as we lay on the grass staring up into the sky yet knowing that with a simple change of perspective we could see all the lights of Brighton and Hove lining the boundary between land and sea.

You may have realized that we have entered a phase of single-word titles for each of our events. We decided to challenge ourselves by setting out a programme of one-word events without knowing what the content of those events might be. The titles were Reflection, Vistas, Drought and Refreshment and each of these titles was chosen and advertised without any pre-determined subject matter; we just had to be on our toes when we started to discuss ideas for the evening.

From Vistas we moved on to Drought and we understood right from the start that while this is about absence of something, usually water, it could equally refer to a lack of community, loss of a particular element or barrenness of some kind or other. When thinking about faith, drought could be used to describe the loss of a feeling that God was present, or a pattern of spiritual aridity which is often experienced by Christians, along with the guilt that often accompanies it. In particular, it is often the case that bad news, whether personal or national, can give individuals a feeling that God is not present and that the world is going to hell in a handbasket. Quite often with a drought the individual is aware of their need but may not know how to go about fulfilling it: at a basic level I may know I need water but don't know where I can get any. These were all starting points for our discussion on how to shape the event.

We wanted to begin by creating an environment of absence by removing everything from the room – slightly problematic in the upper room of a pub which was full of furniture, but we managed to pile all the tables and chairs into an alcove at one end of the bar and covered them all with a black cloth. To engender a feeling that God was absent we covered the floor with pages from newspapers featuring bad-news stories – these weren't hard to find as that's generally the only kind of reports that newspapers carry. As a nod to the traditional understanding of drought being something to do with the desert, we placed a pile of dry pebbles in the centre of the room.

This meant that people had nowhere to sit when they entered the room except on the floor, and to emphasize the drought theme, we also denied them access to the bar so that they couldn't get themselves a drink. The picture on screen was an archetypal desert image of sand and rocks that dissolved into a definition of drought as scarcity, lack, want, dearth, paucity, famine. We then moved on to a brilliant song by Tom Waits called 'God's Away on Business' which I'd coupled with images

of homelessness, famine, flood, wildfire, earthquake and war. It was a pretty bleak start!

Red marker pens were handed out and everyone was asked to look at the news articles under their feet and circle those stories which appeared to them to be 'Godless'. The psalms have a lot to say about God's absence and so someone read Psalm 42:

> As the deer longs for streams of water, so I long for you, O God.
>
> I thirst for God, the living God. When can I go and stand before him?
>
> Day and night I have only tears for food, while my enemies continually taunt me, saying, 'Where is this God of yours?'
>
> My heart is breaking as I remember how it used to be: I walked among the crowds of worshippers, leading a great procession to the house of God, singing for joy and giving thanks amid the sound of a great celebration!
>
> Why am I discouraged? Why is my heart so sad? I will put my hope in God!
>
> I will praise him again – my Saviour and my God!

Now I am deeply discouraged, but I will remember you – even from distant Mount Hermon, the source of the Jordan, from the land of Mount Mizar. I hear the tumult of the raging seas as your waves and surging tides sweep over me. But each day the LORD pours his unfailing love upon me, and through each night I sing his songs, praying to God who gives me life.
'O God my rock', I cry, 'Why have you forgotten me? Why must I wander around in grief, oppressed by my enemies?' Their taunts break my bones. They scoff, 'Where is this God of yours?'
Why am I discouraged? Why is my heart so sad? I will put my hope in God! I will praise him again – my Saviour and my God!
(NLT)

We wanted people to think about how close or far they felt from God without putting them on the spot or asking them to reveal something very personal to a room full of strangers, and we hit upon the idea of using the rocks. Attendees were invited to take a pebble from the pile in the middle and move it to a place in the room which represented their relationship to God – we set no scale to this and allowed people to make their own decision about how the room and the starting point related to distance to or from God and their placement of a pebble.

This was followed by a short reading from Pete Rollins' book *The Orthodox Heretic* and his re-titling of the well-known parable as the Prodigal Father, a story of a son who distances himself from his father who never stops loving him anyway. John Bell was next in an audio clip where he talks about Jesus' words on the cross, 'My God, my God, why have you forsaken me?'. John explains that being abandoned by God is a normal human experience which we almost all undergo, and that for Jesus to be truly human he also had to experience this. To reinforce the universal truth of this absence we then moved to consider some mystical writers of the Middle Ages in words by St John of the Cross and a section from *The Cloud of Unknowing*:

My mind became dimmed in a strange way; no truth seemed clear to me.
When people spoke to me about God, my heart was like a rock. I could not draw from it a single sentiment of love for Him.
When I tried, by an act of the will, to remain close to Him, I experienced great torments, and it seemed to me that I was only provoking God to an even greater anger.
... I felt in my soul a great void, and there was nothing with which I could fill it. I began to suffer from a great hunger and yearning for God, but I saw my utter powerlessness.
(St John of the Cross)

And if ever you come to this cloud, and make a home there and take up the work of love as I urge you, there is something else you must do as this cloud is above you, and between you and your God, you must put a cloud of forgetting beneath you, between you and all the creatures that have ever been made.

The cloud of unknowing will perhaps leave you with a feeling that you are far from God. But I assure you, if it is authentic, only the absence of a cloud of forgetting between you and all creatures keeps you from God. (*The Cloud of Unknowing*)

This demonstrated that for centuries, people have experienced many of the same emotions and separation from God that we sometimes think of as being unique to modern life.

After listening to all these examples and explanations of how human beings often feel that God is far away, we then asked people to do something. I always think it is important for people to undertake some sort of physical action as it embodies the spiritual in a way that mere discussion or contemplation cannot. They were asked to return to the pebble they had placed on the floor and to rip away the newspaper underneath their rock. When they did this, they found that under the newspaper was more paper and the word 'God' typed out thousands and thousands of times and completely lining the whole floor of the pub. Wherever a hole was made in the newspaper, it was filled with God repeated many, many times. Without realizing it everyone in the room had been sitting on and close to God, even though their thoughts had been entirely directed to God's absence. The projector screen at this point was showing the words 'God is nowhere', which slowly animated to say 'God is now here'.

As a final cleansing act we all pulled up the newspaper pages, leaving a beautiful uniform floor covered in the word 'God' in tiny newsprint style, replacing the chaotic bad news of the world of newspapers with the good news that God is the foundation of all being, underlying everything we do, whether we know it or not. The evening finished on an upbeat note with an image of the famous painting by Salvador Dali, *Christ of St John of the Cross*, and the words 'God is now here' emblazoned beneath it.

Much more appropriate for a pub setting was the final event in this season, which was entitled 'Refreshment'. Pubs rely on providing food as well as drink in order to be financially viable, and eating and drinking together is an important social activity which we reflect symbolically whenever we celebrate communion. So that became the endgame for our evening, to finish with some form of celebration of communion as a sign of spiritual and social refreshment.

On entering the room, attendees found a sumptuous feast of food laid out on a central table with piles of fruit in glittering bowls, platters of bread and cheese, glasses and decanters of wine lit by candles in golden candlesticks. The projector screen was playing a loop of imagery of people splashing around in water set to the Bobby Darin hit 'Splish Splash' from 1958, which set a lovely upbeat tone to the evening. We continued the party theme by asking everyone to join in a game of 'Who am I?'. Every person had a sticker attached to their back with the name of an inspirational person written on it, and they had to try and find out who this was by asking others simple 'yes' or 'no' questions. This had the added advantage of mixing up the group so that people got to meet others unknown to them before the evening began.

After a jovial ten minutes or so playing this game, we all sat at small tables that were scattered around the central feast to talk about people who inspire and invigorate us. These could be personal friends or family, or well-known figures such as writers, speakers or spiritual leaders. As these discussions developed everyone was introduced to the concept of water writing. This uses a product designed to help those learning Chinese calligraphy, which is written using a brush. The person simply dips a paintbrush in water and writes on a special cloth which turns grey wherever the water touches it. After a few minutes, as the water dries, the calligraphy disappears leaving the cloth clean to be used again. Participants were asked to write the name of the person who inspired them most using this technique, hopefully reinforcing the idea that these people refresh our spirits with their inspirational gifts.

After this period of introduction and discussion we wanted to provide some input, and after watching a short slow-motion video of my son as a baby splashing around in a paddling pool which was shot on Super 8 film and looked like it had been filmed in the 1940s, we moved on to listening to some words from scripture.

We decided the story of Jesus' discussion with the Samaritan woman at the well in John 4 was the most appropriate for the evening. Often during planning discussions in preparation for an event, ideas are tabled and then thrown out later on; it can be painful to work in this way as ideas are precious to those who conceive them, but it's a necessary part of the process of refining and honing an event to ensure that everything is directed towards the key objectives of the evening.

To give people a chance to reflect on the concept of living water we wanted to show some work by the video artist Bill Viola, who has created some arresting art featuring people being drenched with water or submerged in slow motion. He has a particularly thrilling installation in St Paul's cathedral on the themes of earth, air, fire and water which I highly recommend to anyone visiting that church. Quite rightly as a video artist his work is carefully protected and at that time could not simply be found on YouTube or other streaming platforms, but we were able to show some stills from one of his artworks called 'Crossing', which features a man being inundated under a waterfall. These videos are now much more readily available on YouTube as are various others of his artworks, many of which have extremely religious themes.

Up to this point we had spent a third of our time together considering emotional refreshment through people who inspire us, another third thinking about spiritual refreshment in relation to God, and we wanted to spend the final third in practical refreshment by sharing the food and drink. I said a simple form of communion, using the words of institution in 1 Corinthians 11, and broke bread and poured out some wine and invited everyone to dig in! The food on the central table was distributed around the smaller tables in the room and little social groups continued to chatter and eat for the rest of our time together. We all recognized that food nourishes our bodies, while the company of others feeds our emotional selves, and the spirit of God works through it all to feed us spiritually. There was a sociable buzz about the space and a feeling of genuine connectedness among us all at the conclusion of the evening.

Moving an artistic spiritual event into a pub is good for those of us who create these events because it makes us think differently

about how we do things and takes us outside the confines of church thinking, which is just as important as the physical act of getting out of church. Pub management is often amenable to the idea of outside groups coming in to run small events, especially at times such as Sunday evenings that are not very busy for them. Many pubs have a function room of some sort that can either be hired for a small fee or booked free on the understanding that attendees will buy drinks. Having an additional 20 or 30 people buying drinks on a quiet Sunday night is quite attractive to managers trying to drum up more business and it's worth mentioning this if the landlord wants to charge a fee.

To make the event truly public some careful thought needs to be put into how it is to be promoted. Many organizations have email lists or link-ups to followers or friends through social media but the challenge is to get publicity out beyond these echo chambers to a wider group who might be interested in the topics you choose for the events. An obvious solution is to put some publicity in the place where the event is being held. A poster in the pub or promotional beer mats will reach anyone coming in for a drink, with the potential that they might engage with your event.

Things to consider

- Remember that pubs are not necessarily helpful venues for those in recovery or with addiction issues.
- Use the conviviality of a pub to encourage further discussion outside the actual event itself.
- Programme planning need be no more than a set of headlines as long as you're confident your team can rise to the challenge of creating something from this simple start.
- Be careful not to ask questions of attendees which could put them on the spot in some way, especially when enquiring about understanding personal faith.
- Try to create an opportunity for some sort of physical/symbolic action.
- When discussing ideas try not to be too precious about them as part of the process will involve discarding ideas that don't fit.

Festival Services

Although I live by the sea I don't really do the whole sea swimming thing, in fact I'm not a massive fan of swimming anywhere because I'm not very confident in water and the sea frightens me with its vastness, roughness and unpredictability. I am hugely admiring of those who swim in it every day and particularly those who engage in sea sports such as surfing, paddleboarding and diving. So I was slightly daunted when we had an approach in 2010 to create an early-morning service for surfers as part of a major festival that runs in Brighton every year.

Paddle Round the Pier began in 1996 when 70 people got together to raise funds for the charity Surfers Against Sewage, and has grown to become a weekend-long festival celebrating all kinds of sea sports with anything up to 55,000 people attending, which now claims to be the world's biggest charity beach and watersports festival. The weekend includes a whole variety of swimming, surfing, paddling and kayaking races as well as home-made raft races, life-saving classes and a big educational programme for young people in the run-up to the event. There is also a large festival village with a performance stage for bands, cafés, bars and restaurants and a whole collection of exhibitors, from companies selling anything from wetsuits to hot tubs, and of course surfboards.

The organizers heard about Beyond, probably through someone telling them about the Beach Hut Advent Calendar, and they contacted me to ask if we'd be interested in running a service at the beginning of the Sunday of the weekend. I was impressed that the organizers had thought about this and wanted to give space for some spirituality during the weekend, and subsequently

learnt that surfing is quite a spiritual activity for many participants. I'd never been invited to do something like this before but
I thought it was a great opportunity to flex our creative muscles
in a new environment and so I said yes.

I recognized right from the start that expecting many people,
especially surfers who had probably been up until late the night
before, to come out early on Sunday was a bit of a challenge, but
the festival programme did begin at 9 a.m. and they offered us
an 8.30 slot for our service. In order to have some impact beyond
that early-morning start, I also thought we should create some
sort of interactive art installation that could remain in place all
day so that the impact of our presence at the festival would be
felt by more than just the early risers.

The Beyond team had a meeting to throw around some ideas
and we decided that we wanted to create some sort of shrine in
the shape of a cross using surfing gear, so I began the process of
trying to beg or borrow some surf kit – as I'm sure you realize
by now I don't possess any of my own! This turned out to be
quite easy as at the western end of Hove is a watersports lagoon
where Lagoon Watersports run year-round classes on windsurfing, water skiing, paddleboarding and so on. They also sell a
lot of equipment, so I approached them to see if they could help
and amazingly it turned out they had a whole store of old para-
phernalia that they wanted to get rid of, so very quickly I found
myself in possession of a huge surfboard, a couple of fibreglass
masts and some old sails.

Alongside planning to create this installation I also had to put
together a short order of service – but where to start? Not long
after moving to Brighton I was invited to join the Hove Deep Sea
Anglers club by some friends who had taken us along as guests a
few times. The Danglers, as it is known colloquially, has a clubhouse right on the beach at the west end of Hove and I had been
there a number of times with my wife for drinks, and as far as I
was concerned it was a social club, rather like a working men's
club which happened to be by the sea. Once we were members,
I realized that it is actually a fishing club and members go out
into the English Channel in quite small boats to fish. One of the

annual events that I heard talked about at the bar was a blessing of the boats and this set me thinking about a service of blessing. It didn't feel right to bless the surfers as that was a bit patronizing and potentially there would not be any there that early, so I decided to call it The Blessing of the Surf.

I had already become used to using Bible passages to highlight the importance of creation in some of our other events and so it seemed natural to begin this service with words from Genesis 1 describing the creation of the world up to the point where God separates the waters above from the waters below and the eventual separation of water from the land. This idea of separation also fitted well with the Celtic concept of thin places (see Chapter 10). These can be actual places, and notoriously are often natural locations, especially where there is a physical margin, for example between land and sea, between sea and sky and between land and sky. But they can also be spiritual or emotional borders, times in our lives when we cross a threshold of some sort, encounter a life-changing event or when circumstances point us in a different direction. Thin places can also be places of holy significance, pilgrimage sites, ancient places of prayer or just places that are special to us because some spiritual awakening has happened there.

I want liturgy to be interactive in some way and so I thought it would be good to have a few minutes for attendees to share any experiences they might have of thin places, especially as they relate to being by the sea or the surf. I found quotes by Albert Einstein and Gandhi about indefinable and mysterious power outside of ourselves, something which some surfer friends had expressed to me in conversations about the experience of being out on the sea. I also found a surfer's code which expressed really well the community that so many value as part of this sport:

The Surfer's Code
I will never turn my back on the ocean
I will paddle back out
I will take the drop with commitment
I will know that there will always be another wave

I will realize that all surfers are joined by one ocean
I will paddle around the impact zone
I will never fight a rip tide
I will watch out for other surfers after a big set
I will pass on my stoke to a non-surfer
I will ride, and not paddle in to shore
I will catch a wave every day, even in my mind
I will honour the sport of kings.

This felt like something that we should all say together, whether we were surfers or not, and was followed by a short thanksgiving for the oceans before ending with a blessing which I based on a well-known Irish prayer:

May the surf rise to meet you,
may the waves be ever at your back,
may all your wave-riding be ever joyous
and until we meet again
may God hold you and your board
in the palm of his hand.
Amen.

This became the basis of an annual Blessing of the Surf service, which we have run most years since 2010 until the advent of Covid, with additions and variations added every year so as to keep this liturgy fresh and alive. I found writing a liturgy like this was relatively straightforward and it was often done as a fairly last-minute thing because most of my energy was focused on the art installation as I knew that thousands of people would be prompted to think about something spiritual if we got this right.

Now that I had plenty of surfing junk, we needed to work out how to turn it into an installation that would arrest the attention of passing festival goers and point them towards something spiritual. The obvious thing to do was to construct some sort of cross with this. We had a tall fibreglass mast for the vertical pole and windsurf booms either side formed the cross shape, and we found that by turning the sails upside down we could reinforce the whole structure so that it stayed cross-shaped. To complete it and to give it some structural strength the surfboard was lashed to the vertical mast and this then formed a blank canvas for some graphic work.

The image that immediately came to mind was one which had appeared on the ruined West Pier and that was dear to my heart as a perfect piece of site-specific graffiti. The West Pier had been in ruinous decline since before we moved to Hove in 1999 and was irreparably damaged in 2003 by a series of fires which sealed its fate as a hopeless case that could not be restored. There is still a considerable hulk remaining to this day that is slowly being eroded away by time and tide. In 2010 I noticed that someone had spray-graffitied a simple 'Jesus' face onto one of the pier supports which now stood alone on the beach, keeping watch over the rest of the ruin as it stretched out to sea. The genius of the placement was that it was just beneath a ring of spikes that had been added to the pillar to stop people climbing up it when it was originally part of the pier. Barbed wire was also wound around these spikes to create a perfect crown of thorns on the forehead of the spray-painted face of Jesus. I subsequently discovered that this artwork had been created by an Italian street-art duo called Orticanoodles who had visited Brighton, seen this rusting opportunity and created a brilliant piece of art.

I used one of the many photos I had taken of this to create my own stencil and after a bit of practice on various pieces of wood and card felt confident enough to spray my version of this face onto the surfboard at approximately the height that a head would be if the board was a human body. So the constituent pieces of our installation were ready but we weren't entirely sure how it was all going to look once assembled, as our piece was also going to be site specific and couldn't be put together until the actual day.

So on 4 July 2010, a small team set off early for the beach with masts, booms, sails, a surfboard, ropes, duct tape and anything else we could think of that might be needed to make this work. We selected a spot near the starting line for the various races that were due to be run that day and quite quickly managed to put the whole artwork together and lash it to the railings on the seafront. The only problem was that, as is so often the case, there was a pretty strong wind coming in from the sea that day and the sails caught the wind beautifully and the whole thing was in danger of being blown over. Not to be deterred we added guy ropes and weights and anything else we could find to make it as safe as possible as we weren't planning on attending for the whole day and we didn't want it to blow over on top of anyone. Hitting people over the head with our message didn't seem like a very good idea!! It also taught me the necessity of having insurance and doing risk assessments when setting things up in public!

Once installed, this made a great backdrop for our first Blessing of the Surf service. A dozen or so people joined our little set-up team and we read, prayed and reflected in the beautiful early-morning sunlight. It doesn't matter to me that only a small number of people turned up; the important thing was that the day was blessed, the event was prayed for, and whether they knew it or not, all the participants and visitors to the festival that day had been committed to God. This is the value of being faithful in prayer and worship in churches and homes wherever they may be and however many are participating; it is the intentional placing of the day into a divine context.

The final piece of the jigsaw was to add something to the installation for people to respond to. Some of the liturgy was taped to the surfboard inviting passers-by to stop and reflect for a few moments on the wonders of creation that were being celebrated on the seafront that day. At the foot of the surfers' cross we created a cairn of white pebbles and attached some marker pens to the railings with long strings and a notice by the stones encouraging people to write some thoughts or concerns or names of loved ones on a stone and cast these into the sea as a way of committing that thought to God.

As a newly licensed parish priest I then had a busy morning running services at my church and so we left the installation to take its chances with the public. The earliest I was able to return was the middle of that afternoon and I was relieved to find that the installation had survived. It was deviating a bit from its original upright stance but hadn't fallen on anyone and it only took a few moments to tighten the guy ropes and straighten it up. Most exciting was that the cairn of white pebbles had almost disappeared and instead there was a pile of white stones scattered on the beach below with various names inscribed on them as people had responded to the call to pray for friends and family in this creative way.

2011 came round and in preparation for being asked to do this again we planned a suite of events themed around the four elements, Fire, Earth, Water and Air, and billing the water event as our contribution to Paddle Round the Pier. The Beyond team took one of the quotes from the Blessing of the Surf liturgy as the starting point for the art: 'When you look at yourself from a universal standpoint, something inside always reminds or informs you that there are bigger and better things to worry about' (often attributed to Albert Einstein).

This led to the creation of a small reflection pool made from a little aquarium with mirrors on the floor under the water, on which were written a series of questions that hopefully provoked people into thinking about how they saw themselves, compared to how others might see them. Included was Jesus' question from Luke chapter 9, when he asks, 'Who do you say I am?', encouraging people to broaden their horizons a little, considering how their views relate to God. Visitors were asked to contribute to the installation by writing about what they had seen in their reflection, or to contribute thoughts of their own.

Once again this was set up before the service, which used the same liturgy as the year before, and this time we were joined by a few members of the Christian Surfers organization, who had a stand in the festival village and who subsequently became important partners in this work. They were able to keep an eye on the art installation during the day and found it a really helpful discussion starter for people who stopped to look at it. In the evening some team members came back to pack up the installation and collect the responses that people had contributed during the day. These included: 'I like my reflection', 'I am finally learning the meaning of self-love', 'Make sure that you make time to reflect' and 'I'm so happy to be alive'.

Early on in the life of Beyond I got a bit obsessed with ice sculptures (see Chapters 2 and 3) and in the course of extensive exploration and research involving purchasing second-hand chest freezers, discovered that home-made ice is very dull and grey and gets stuck as it expands. Filling our garden with old white goods and incurring the wrath of my wife spurred me on to find a trade supplier who could provide inexpensive beautiful clear ice not too far away from Brighton. Their foundation product was a 1 metre by 0.5 metre by 0.25 metre block of crystal-clear ice and in the past I had created simple sculptures from this building block, so as to keep the costs as low as possible, because the expensive part of commissioning an ice sculpture is asking it to be carved into a shape of some kind.

For the next Blessing of the Surf art installation I had a vision for an ice psalm. This would be three of the standard blocks placed on top of each other to create three layers – the undersea world, the surface of the sea and the sky above. Under the sea we would place various multi-coloured fish and sea creatures, on the surface of the sea would be surfers and swimmers reflecting the activities of the festival, and floating above them in the sky would be some words from the psalms.

I booked the ice company to create these blocks and made all the arrangements for the finished piece to be delivered to Brighton early on Sunday morning in a refrigerated truck, and then began the process of finding the objects to place in the ice. Finding plastic fish and fake seaweed was easy as they could be sourced from any aquarium shop. But tracking down appropriate-sized human figures proved remarkably difficult. For the scale to work I wanted figurines that were smaller than an Action Man or Barbie (which wouldn't have been right anyway) but bigger than commonly available model people such as those used by architects. Eventually I found a model-railway superstore in Sussex and so I set off in the hope that they would have something I could use.

This opened up a completely new world to me as I discovered that there are a whole variety of gauges of sizes of figurines to match different types of model railway. The size that suited my planned sculpture turned out to be G scale – figures that are 7–12 cm high; the variety of situations and characters that are available is extraordinary. I would highly recommend anyone interested who has spare time to visit the Walthers.com website if you're ever looking for inspiration about different walks of life. Among the left-handed gunmen, groups of rather flirty-looking female passers-by or religious sets with a priest and a full complement of altar servers, I managed to find a group of swimmers and some sunbathers that were perfect or which we could adapt slightly for our purposes.

One of our team was able to make some suitably sized surfboards to go with the figurines and I set off for the ice makers with the fish, the people and some ideas for surf as well as some words to go in the sky. The process of embedding items in the ice is fairly straightforward as each ice block grows from the bottom of a 1 metre by 0.5 metre trough at the rate of about 2 cm per day, taking 10–12 days to become a fully-formed block. Items are placed in the trough once there are a couple of centimetres of ice already formed and weighted down until they're secured by the growing ice.

The undersea block was very straightforward as the fish and seaweed were just placed in at random. The middle block needed some surf and the ice supplier suggested we try opaque florist's cellophane and so I brought some with me. We scrunched this up and placed it at the bottom of the surface layer, weighted down so that it wouldn't float, and also placed some of the swimming/ surfing figures among the folds and left the ice to do its work and grow up around them. I thought the sky would be easy as I had printed some verses from the psalms on acetate and had planned that these could just be placed in the ice. Unfortunately, we discovered inkjet printing on acetate dissolves in water! So two days after my visit I got a call from the ice supplier to say that the acetate was now completely clear and all the words had disappeared! Time was getting tight so in a panic I printed the verses in a variety of different formats including laser printing, inkjet and then laminating, and even using good old-fashioned overhead projector slides. I tested these in a bowl of water before sending over the ones that seemed to be most stable and hoped for the best. To my relief I got a call the next day saying this was all fine and the words were still visible as they became encased in ice.

The Sunday of the festival came and as usual we were up early so as to be on the seafront in time for the refrigeration truck and to check that we had all the right passes and permissions from the festival. At 8 a.m. the truck arrived and manoeuvred into position, opening up the doors to reveal our sculpture wrapped in plastic and resting on a pallet.

Once installed in place on the plinth we had prepared we removed the covering and for the first time got sight of our creation, which surpassed all our expectations. The blue-green ice sparkled in the early-morning light, revealing a wonderfully coloured undersea world and amazingly life-like surf with surfers and bathers nestled among the bubbly folds of waves. Above it all, floating ethereally in the sky, like clouds sent from God, were the words we had chosen from the psalms: 'The earth is full of God's glory as the waters cover the sea', 'I am the Lord your God, I stir up the ocean. I make its waves roar', 'Let the oceans and everything that moves in them praise the Lord.' The whole installation far surpassed our hopes and expectations and the instant it was unveiled it began to attract attention from those walking past.

At that moment I felt the presence of God on that beach and was grateful for this opportunity for epiphany. Doing this kind of work not only touches the public who happen across events like this but affects and informs our own faith. Throughout the years that I have run Beyond and created installations, events and services, I have gained as much as anyone through this work and my faith has grown and deepened and changed as a result. It's incredibly rewarding and a good enough reason in itself to engage in this kind of expression of what we believe, irrespective of whether it affects anyone else.

As usual we held our Blessing of the Surf service with the ice psalm as a kind of altar in the world and focus for our worship. Then the Christian Surfers took over as they opened up their stand which was nearby, and they made sure that someone was stationed near the sculpture to chat to anyone who was interested. One of the things that happens when an ice sculpture is placed in direct sunlight is that as well as melting it very quickly begins to craze. In this case it began at the top of the sculpture, which made it look as though clouds were descending on the whole scene, encouraging people to come closer to peer into the fog to see the messages from God.

The artwork was a huge draw for the crowds throughout the day as people wanted to see the imagery embedded in the ice and children wanted to touch it and feel the coolness during the heat of the day. Despite this being a beautiful sunny July day, the English sun was not strong enough to melt the whole sculp-

ture, and when we came back at 7 p.m. to clear up, we found an appreciably big lump of ice still there but almost all the figurines had disappeared, leaving behind two swimmers, a surfboard and the remains of an arm and most of one leg. Like holy relics from an ancient shrine, I collected these up and have kept them to this day as a reminder that God was present on the seafront that day, speaking to thousands of people.

Since that highpoint at the festival our presence has had its highs and lows. One year we planned to chalk a labyrinth onto the promenade but the day turned out to be rain-filled and a wash-out, making it impossible to chalk anything onto the tarmac and so after the early-morning service we abandoned everything. The next time we returned, the surfboard from the very first Blessing of the Surf made a reappearance as the 'Surfboard of Prayer'. It was mounted upright against one of the fences surrounding the festival village and inscribed on it was a simple invitation for people to write prayers on the board using the pens provided.

Another year I was inspired by the idea of creating a human sundial as an interactive way of getting people to think about time and the passing of each day. Throughout May and June, I spent an inordinate amount of time in our garden with a large white piece of card, a stick and a compass marking out the place-ment of the shadow at various times of day to form the basis of the sundial. I'm sure you can appreciate that this was a bit hit and miss due to the vagaries of the English weather and the avail-ability of sunlight on any given day! I also had to try and account for the fact that the sun changes position month by month and to estimate where it was going to be on the first Sunday in July.

The day for the festival came and the team headed to the beach early once more, armed with plenty of rolls of white duct tape, my sundial card template and the compass. It was cloudy when we arrived and it wasn't possible to take a reading from the sun, so we had to set about marking out the sundial in faith that my calculations were correct – not a certainty by any means! We chose a central point and extrapolated long lines from my template using pieces of white tape. At the end of each line, we taped a sheet with the time and at the base of all these lines was

a notice saying, 'This is a human sundial, stand on this spot and your shadow should indicate the time.' Placed around the whole installation we also taped more signs with various Bible verses from Jeremiah, Isaiah, Habakkuk and the psalms (again!).

Having laid out the whole installation in faith we then proceeded to hold our Blessing of the Surf service, which I had adapted to suit the theme and began with the standard opening to Morning Prayer:

The night has passed, and the day lies open before us;
let us pray with one heart and mind.
Silence is kept.
As we rejoice in the gift of this new day,
so may the light of your presence, O God,
set our hearts on fire with love for you;
now and for ever.
Amen.

We brought the service to a close with these words:

May every SUNRISE hold more PROMISE
And every SUNSET hold more PEACE.
Amen.

At which point the sun suddenly appeared from behind the clouds. One of the teenagers in our group raced to the central spot of the sundial and raised her arms to form a point and to my delight and relief her shadow pointed to the exact correct time! Never have I felt the word 'hallelujah' to be more appropriate! This prompted everyone to have a go at being the 'hands' of the sundial and we left hoping that it would keep accurate time throughout the day.

Returning at 8 p.m. that night to clear everything away we found people still using the installation to enjoy seeing their shadow tell the time and to take photos of themselves as part of this illustration of the divine rhythm of a day – and it was still telling the time accurately!

What was to be the last installation as a result of Covid was entitled 'The Cleansing Pool', and once again the day turned out to be wet and windy but I'd learnt my lesson and the artwork wasn't so weather dependent. It consisted of a large paddling pool surrounded by little piles of white pebbles, with signs all around it. What I hadn't anticipated was the amount of water that was needed to fill the pool and how difficult that would be as we had to lug it in carriers from the only tap available, which was about 200 yards away. Once it had a decent amount of water in it, I was tempted to get in to cleanse myself after all that hard work! The signs around the pool said:

THE CLEANSING POOL
Water is a potent spiritual symbol which can mean many different things. The Christian tradition often associates water with the cleansing of our lives from all the grubby messiness of daily life which the Bible calls sin.

As a cleansing act you can write your name or make a mark on one of the pebbles around this pool and put the pebble in the water. The marker pens are non-permanent so the marks will eventually be washed away.

'Clean the slate, God, so we can start the day fresh! Keep me from stupid sins, from thinking I can take over your work; Then I can start this day sun-washed, scrubbed clean of the grime of sin.' Psalm 19.12–13 (*The Message*)

Returning at the end of the day we found the pool filled with pebbles. Many were blank, many had smudges of messages left after being in the water all day, many had just names and some had messages, including 'Miss you mum', 'God save the world' and 'Help the homeless'.

There are all sorts of festivals happening in all sorts of places throughout the year and I believe it's possible to shape something appropriate with a Christian heart for all situations. There may not be something as big as a surf festival or music festival near you, but there will be local events such as summer fairs, street parties or food festivals. All over the country there are special events unique to a particular locality that could provide an opportunity for a blessing of some sort: a cheese-rolling day, a scarecrow festival or a bog snorkelling event; these all provide an opportunity for some form of creative Christian engagement.

If you're already involved in helping to organize one of these then it's relatively easy to suggest an interactive installation as part of the day or to programme in a short service of blessing at the beginning if you feel confident in doing that. If you're not one of the organizers then you can make a gentle approach to those who are, with some suggestions that would add content and enhance the day; people are usually keen for anything that would add interest to their festival as long as it doesn't require any extra work from them. Assure the organizers that it would be no trouble to them and would fit with the ethos of the festival, and promise to review it with them afterwards if they would like that.

Practically, make sure you have enough people to carry off your idea, as well as a checklist of all the things you will need, but most of all make sure you have a good idea. I am often asked how I come up with ideas, so here are some tips for concept creation that I hope you will find useful.

Like all the best things in life, this is best done with a small group of people you know and trust, but can just as easily be achieved on your own; it's just more fun in a group. The first thing to remember is that there are no bad ideas. Edward de Bono has a scheme for creative thinking where he suggests people wear imaginary hats in various colours and the one hat you must banish from the room is the black hat – this is the judge. This is the voice that says, 'We tried that before and it didn't work' or 'We can't afford it' or 'It's not Christian enough'. Don't worry about any of that; you can tease out those sorts of issues later on. The key to generating good ideas is not to care. For information about the other five hats and how to use them, go to www.edwarddebono.com.

The next thing is to go for quantity not quality; throw out as many ideas in as short a time as possible – ideally with someone scribbling them down. It's far better to have 20 crazy, impossible, diverse ideas in five minutes than five 'good' ideas in 20 minutes. It's often good to start with simple word association – pick a single word, 'surf' or 'cheese' or 'scarecrow' or 'summer' or 'God' – and get people to shout out the first word that comes to mind. Jot these down as a word cloud on a big sheet of paper or using a flip chart, and if suggestions begin to flag then pick one of the secondary words and start again with that one. Keep going until you have three or four pages of random words and then start to review those and see if any of them begin to solidify into a concept.

Invariably, randomly suggested words will provoke discussion and begin to coalesce into more fully-formed ideas, and you can let these discussions develop once you've got a full page of words. Alternatively, you can let the discussion progress a little, then park it for a fuller discussion later. Sometimes people will need to give some context to particular words they blurt out and that may well become the core of a project.

This kind of idea generation does need someone to moderate or be the instigator, someone who is prepared to move discussion on quickly when necessary, make suggestions about lines of thought as they arise and understand when a particular concept could be fruitful for more detailed examination.

As the group begins to home in on a specific idea then generally it is helpful to have one person take ownership of the idea and flesh it out so the detail has been thought through. Often this will mean someone going away and writing up the concept a little more fully, and then a second meeting to decide who is going to do what, how and when, and to allocate responsibilities and tasks so that the idea actually gets done.

Things to consider

- Cultivate relationships with other organizations who run events which might allow an opportunity for you to create something.
- Seize every opportunity offered to you, no matter how far outside your comfort zone this might be.
- Consider how to establish a presence throughout the duration of the festival without necessarily involving team members' attendance.
- Don't worry too much about attendance numbers; it's the quality of involvement that counts.
- Give yourself time to experiment if your artistic idea involves some technical know-how.
- Outdoor activities need to take account of the potential weather and you should have a reserve plan if it's terrible!
- Do risk assessments and make sure you have public liability insurance.
- Practise having idea sessions; the brain is like a muscle, it works best when it's exercised regularly.

12

Holy Huts

As mentioned right at the beginning of this book, beach huts have been an excellent anchor point for creative installations, but you don't need a beach or a hut to be able to try some of these ideas in your own setting. The great thing that a beach hut does is provide a focus that is both fully public but which also is a legitimate reason for being present. It's hard just to set up an installation in the middle of a field or a shopping street without some sort of base from which to operate, even if it's as simple as a table, some signage or even just a chair.

After years of being present on the seafront every day in December experiencing snow, rain, wind, cold and the occasional beautiful clear day, I longed to do something at a more temperate time of year. Beach huts have a shrine-like quality to their design, reminding me of the little wayside tabernacles you sometimes come across in southern Mediterranean countries such as Greece. These two thoughts merged when I was thinking about the week running up to Easter and how to help people understand something about Holy Week.

The Holy Week Hut would be a series of installations starting on the Monday before Easter and running up to the Saturday, focusing on different aspects of the Easter story in creative ways, like a springtime version of the Beach Hut Advent Calendar. Rather than moving up and down the seafront we decided the same hut would be open for an hour at sunset every day as there are usually people strolling along the seafront at that time.

I took the principal themes of stations of the cross and combined them into six topics for the artists to focus on with their installations; these were Judgement, Burden, Failure, Compassion,

Persecution and Death. Each night we had a different guest artist who created the installation in their own unique style, and two or three volunteers came to sit at the hut, talk to those who stopped by, and towards the end of the hour share a simple meal of bread and wine as part of our witness and remembrance of Jesus.

The Easter story begins with Jesus being condemned to death by Pilate, hence the theme of judgement for this first holy hut. A couple of years before this I had installed a mirror completely covering the back wall of our hut as part of one of the advent calendar installations and the artist made full use of this to help us think about our judgement of others. We saw our own image reflected in the mirrored back wall of the hut being watched by a large pair of eyes that had been painted onto it. The legend 'First take the log out of your own eye and then you will be able to see clearly to take the speck out of your brother's eye' was written on the bottom of the mirror. All around the hut was a display of transcripts of critical quotes from social media in response to a video performance that had been posted online.

One of the issues that we'd never had to deal with before was that of authenticity and offence. A few of the social media quotes on display used quite offensive words, which was why they were appropriate for this installation as they reminded us of how Jesus was abused and taunted by the soldiers. But this was a public installation at 5.30 p.m. in the afternoon and there would be families with children passing by, possibly coming specifically to see the hut and I felt we shouldn't be subjecting them to this kind of language. Fortunately, I had a black marker pen with me and after some discussion with the artist, we agreed to block out the offensive words. The installation was no less effective for this 'censoring' and in a way the blocks of black ink made a point about the fury that is sometimes generated on social media, which can be a very toxic environment. This also made me think about making sure that anything we did from then on was appropriate for all ages.

Burdens was a much less controversial theme and was a very simple idea, straightforward to put together, as it consisted of the hut being entirely filled with stacks of old-style luggage. Leather suitcases, trunks and hat boxes were piled on top of each other, each with a cardboard luggage label with a prayer asking God to help us with our burdens:

Oh my Lord,
I am carrying too much luggage,
And it's weighing me down,
Holding me back.
I worry about losing it,
But I don't need much of the stuff
I am dragging about.
It blocks up aisles and gangways,
Getting in the way,
Making people cross
And wrapping itself round my ankles.
I need to learn to travel light,
But I don't know what to do with all the stuff.

Here,
You take it.
I'm leaving it with you.
Perhaps you can find a better use for it.

You are my unfolding and my unburdening.
You are the keeper of my deepest secrets.

This hut also came with an activity as people who stopped were
invited to take a label and, in privacy, write about their own burdens, which were then burnt on a blazing brázier set up in front
of the hut, symbolizing those burdens being taken away. This
also had the advantage of keeping us warm as even in springtime
it can be pretty cold on Brighton seafront.

Day three of the Holy Week Hut was the day to focus on
failure, a reference to the idea of falling that is such a recurrent
theme in the stations of the cross. The hut was decorated inside
with photographs of people falling, along with a laptop which
was playing a video loop of a series of long queues of people
falling into each other like a set of dominoes. Mirroring this in
front of the hut was a large board set on top of a table with a
black cross marked out on it with duct tape and an invitation to
try and create a domino rally on the cross. This was very hard to
achieve as invariably one of the dominoes would fall or the wind
would blow them or a dog would jog the table, collapsing all
the upended dominoes that had been set up to that point. Everyone who tried this had lots of opportunity to experience failure,
which was the whole point of the task.

At one stage two people began to work together so one of them
held on to a standing domino so as to prevent a collapse while
the other person worked at positioning other dominoes. As soon
as this happened it created a feeling of security for them both and
it all progressed much faster until a full line of pieces was all set
ready to be toppled. The participants commented on how they
felt a sense of relief and relaxation once they started collaborating, which helped with the building. This was a moment of
epiphany as they both realized that working together had helped

to allay their fear of failure – not a bad principle for our lives together.

The weather was not very compassionate for the compassion hut as it was rainy, cold and windy on the seafront – so much for running the event at a more temperate time of year! Fortunately, the artist was ensconced inside the hut with her installation, which was a modern take on Jesus' compassionate act of service to the disciples at the Last Supper. She had a proper shoe-shine chair set up, complete with a little footstool for people to rest their feet on and a whole box of different types of shoe polish and cleaning products. The few people who braved the rain and wind got some respite from the storm as they sat inside the hut to experience this compassionate act of service, mimicking the actions of Jesus which we remember on Maundy Thursday.

Good Friday took the image of a hammer as the central motif as a hammer can be used to drive a nail home or to release it. In the middle of the persecution hut was a piece of timber bristling with nails and one of the team regularly hammered more nails into it as someone read out a story about our propensity to try and nail everything down. We also heard the experience of an artist who plants pansies at the sites of incidents of homophobic abuse to highlight the persecution LGBTQ+ people are often subjected to. Towards the end of the hour we were all invited to come and release a nail from the wood and collect a packet of seeds to plant at a location of our choice as a sign of our commitment to stand up to abuse and persecution. One of the things I think it's important for Christians to do is to call out injustice and prejudice wherever we find it, especially in our own church backyard. We have often found that artists have a keen sense of this and many of the installations created in our various projects have had a political or social conscience as well as a spiritual heart. I believe the two things go together and that Christians shouldn't be afraid to court controversy and discussion about important subjects such as prejudice, inequality and poverty.

Very few followers were prepared to follow Jesus all the way to the cross and there were very few of us at the last holy hut on Easter Eve because the weather was so awful. There is something very appropriate about focusing on death when the wind is howling around and the rain is lashing down, and we had plenty of that on the seafront this day. The art on display was a specially created lithograph of soldiers and poppies reminding us of Remembrance day and Jesus' words: 'Greater love has no one than this, to lay down their life for their friends.' A few hardy souls did make it down to this last event and we huddled in the shelter of the hut as we remembered Christ's death in the sharing of bread and wine. It all felt very difficult, lonely and dispiriting as we thought back to the feelings of those first followers as they tried to process the events of the Friday crucifixion the day after, without knowing that there was going to be a Sunday resurrection. Holy Saturday is a special day for me as it represents an absence of God that is felt by many in their lives. It's a day I often return to when talking to people who are struggling with their faith or with their life circumstances, as it speaks to me of a God who understands the isolation we sometimes feel as human beings.

We learnt a few practical lessons about running an event like this, which helped to inform the shape of the Holy Week Hut project the following year. The first was to pick a hut in a busier location: it's not much good running an event for passers-by if there aren't any! Our first attempt at this was using a hut that was just about the furthest away from the centre of Brighton as you could manage! So for the next Holy Week we secured a location much closer to the city centre and a much more popular part of the seafront for sunset walks. The second lesson was to be a bit more explicit about the connection to the Easter story and so we chose six key parts of the Easter narrative and would focus on one each night. Alongside this we also produced a flyer to be handed out each night which contained the full Easter narrative as the increasing secularization of society means that there is growing ignorance of the Christian story.

The lack of exposure to Bible stories and the Christian narrative is one of the factors we must consider when taking events out into public space. Generally, people know the basic story of Christmas, although this is usually learnt through Christmas carols which are notoriously inaccurate when compared with the biblical accounts, but we cannot assume that people know the Easter story or anything much about Jesus' life, if they know about Jesus at all. I was once doing an interview for a local TV channel about Advent and the beach huts, and halfway through, the interviewer asked if there was anything in the Bible about Jesus! Always start from first principles when organizing something in public and make sure to avoid Christian jargon such as redemption, sanctification or sin; and if you do want to use words such as holy, make sure you know why and that you're able to explain it to any enquirers.

The Monday of Holy Week began with the Last Supper, conveniently forgetting that this story normally gets told on Maundy Thursday. The hut was set for a simple picnic with a table and chairs, a home-baked loaf of bread and some wine glasses. The loaf had a cross shape carved into the crust and two of the wine glasses had been tipped over, spilling their contents onto the white table cloth and forming a stain in the shape of a cross. Attached to one of the glasses was a little label saying, 'To the World, from Jesus Christ, the only Son of God, with all my love.' On getting there I realized that I'd forgotten to bring a sign telling people what this was about, but with some quick thinking the artist was able to write 'The Last Supper' in red wine on a spare tablecloth which we laid in front of the hut.

Day 2 took us to the Garden of Gethsemane and a different artist, who had brought a copy of her favourite painting of an olive grove by Van Gogh. This was mounted on a slanting easel and along the top of it ran a plastic tube that had holes in it. Red wine flowed through the tube and dripped down the face of the painting, reminding us of the drops of blood that Jesus sweated in the garden as he prayed for this cup to pass from him. The installation included a story from the artist, who had found herself crying when she saw the original painting in a gallery and discovered later that although the painting was entitled 'Olive Grove', Van Gogh regarded it as a painting of Gethsemane.

Jesus is betrayed was the theme for day 3 and once again the lipstick-stained shirt and Des'ree track 'Kissing You' were used (see Chapter 6), this time with the shirt mounted on a cross and at the head an image of Jesus kissing Judas taken from a sculpture mounted on the Sagrada Família cathedral in Barcelona. In front of the hut was The Betrayal Box, a large wooden box into which attendees could post written confessions or experiences of betrayal that would then be burnt on Good Friday in an act of absolution and forgiveness. Sheets with a big red lipstick kiss and SWALK (Sealed With A Loving Kiss) were provided, and a number of people took this opportunity, including one woman who used a couple of sheets to write a long story about a friend who had betrayed her, and had a bit of a cry once she'd posted them in the box.

The next instalment of the Easter story was Pilate abdicating responsibility for Jesus' death by washing his hands of him. The hut was decked in banners in various shades of red which were embroidered with the words of Pilate as he sent Jesus off to be crucified. In the middle at the back of the hut was a mysterious figure, also dressed in red, facing away from us. This was Pilate turning his back on the situation; or was it representing us turning our back on Jesus and going our own way? The table outside the hut held a red-stained bowl filled with water and we were all invited to wash our hands while contemplating what we abdicated responsibility for.

Good Friday had to be about the crucifixion and the artist for this day had created a wonderfully expressive collage of Jesus on the cross with head bowed as he contemplated his situation. The rips of the paper echoed the wounds of the whips and there were genuine thorns wired to the canvas as the crown that tore Jesus' flesh and added to the pain of crucifixion. In the background was a soundtrack of rain and rolling thunder as the Gospels describe the land being dark and a storm rising as Jesus came to the end of his life. This hut speaks to us of a God who accompanies us through all the storms of life, even when it seems that he is absent.

We were asked to reflect on Jesus' words on the cross, 'My God, My God, why have you forsaken me?', as it's such an extraordinary statement from the Son of God and it's somehow comforting to know that Jesus echoes the thoughts of so many who suffer and wonder where God is in the midst of their pain. Paradoxically, it gives us hope to think of Jesus experiencing the absence of the divine, Jesus who understands that we too question God's presence sometimes, especially during times of suffering and distress.

The final hut captured the moment of Jesus' death when a mighty storm covered the land, the veil of the temple was torn in two and Jesus yielded up his spirit to God. A pair of white cloths hung in the entrance to the hut, framing a rough-hewn wooden cross made of driftwood from the beach. The bottom of the lengths of linen were stained scarlet as though they had been dipped in blood and 'The veil was torn in two' was chalked on the tarmac between them.

The curtain in the temple separated the holy of holies, where you could be closer to God, from the rest of the temple, which was open to the public. The only person who was allowed to enter the inner sanctum was the high priest who would offer sacrifices on behalf of the people. The tearing of the veil in two symbolically destroyed the barrier between God and humanity. From this moment onwards we all have direct access to God through Jesus' death on the cross and don't have to rely on others to intercede for us. We can now all experience the presence of God and we hoped that people would find that to be true this Easter.

The Holy Week Hut was an attempt to lift the veil on the story of Jesus' passion to a wider audience than the devotees of church who would hear and relive this story through the pattern of services inside churches during that week. There is enormous drama and power in this saga of God enduring suffering and death, identifying with us in our human struggle and helping us to know that we are not alone when we experience the difficulties of life.

Things to consider

- When doing an event in public, give yourself some sort of base: a chair, a banner, a tent or gazebo.
- If you want to attract passers-by, make sure you pick a location with good footfall.
- Make sure your public art is not offensive to anyone.
- Do not assume people know anything about the Bible or Christianity; the stories we know so well may be unfamiliar to them, though they are often willing to hear them.

Conclusion

The aim of this book has been to inspire you to think creatively about your own faith and maybe to take some of these ideas and create your own versions or come up with ideas of your own to help people explore Christian faith in new and creative ways. This can be in a church setting or with support from a faith community, or it could have nothing to do with church but everything to do with God who is much bigger than can be contained within any organization.

This book focuses on developing artistic projects in public spaces, but many people reading it will already have a space available to them for artistic events which is easy to use without the hassle or expense of finding a different venue. These spaces are churches, and they come in an enormous variety of shapes, sizes and types with varying degrees of connection to their local communities and different associations with the idea of being public. Churches and faith groups also often have separate spaces such as halls or a relationship with a community hall, and sometimes there are associated schools with all the resources that they include, which can be very helpful in terms of facilities such as staging, projectors, PA and so on. One of the other advantages of schools is that they also have a built-in audience through the community of families whose children attend.

Many faith groups do amazing things with their buildings and many ministers, lay readers, wardens and congregation members put a lot of time, energy and creativity into making their particular space relevant to their community. Churches host youth clubs and toddler groups, choir concerts and exhibitions, foodbanks, meals for the homeless, recovery groups, counselling services, bookshops and post offices, and these are important resources for their communities and often act as hubs for a whole network of people who don't attend on Sunday or describe themselves as Christian. This care for the souls of the parish is part of the DNA of the Church of England and creates important connections that are the beating heart of a lively church and an engaged Christian faith. It's possible to use these buildings in creative ways to open people's minds and hearts to the possibility of God mediated through art rather than liturgy or worship.

Experiments that we've tried using church buildings have included:

- A photographic exhibition of work created by homeless folk using disposable cameras.
- 'Art from the Edge', which was an exhibition of work by those in recovery, subtitled 'Artwork by and about people on the margins of society'.
- A Jazz Eucharist stretching the understanding of liturgical music into a genre not often represented in church. Similarly, a U2charist using music by the band U2 or a *Les Mis* Mass based on the songs from the popular musical.
- A Maundy Thursday communion supper as a full meal using elements of the Jewish Seder meal and replacing foot washing with more contemporary rituals such as hand sanitizing.
- Various forms of Good Friday meditations using different artistic interpretations of the stations of the cross.
- The Light Eucharist described in Chapter 7 works very well in a church setting.

While I started this book by saying that churches are not proper public spaces, it cannot be doubted that they have the potential to be if we can find ways to make them accessible and approachable for those who are a bit wary of religion. I have come to appreciate that a church building can be a marvellous asset as long as we're not too precious about it and find ways for everyone in the community to feel comfortable about coming in.

Some people would describe Beyond as a 'fresh expression' but I have a problem with that because the Fresh Expressions movement, and to a certain extent the development of pioneer ministry, is mostly about finding new ways to do church. I'm much more interested in helping people to find new ways to believe in God and to love and follow Jesus. That may involve going to church at some point, but the first order of business should always be to introduce people to God in new and creative ways and to help them think about their relationship with the divine, not their understanding of an institution. I think if our only objective is to fill the church pews then we have the wrong focus because it just becomes a marketing campaign with the ever-increasing use of gimmicks to attract people in, which ultimately doesn't have the depth of belief that will sustain faith in God throughout a lifetime.

I also think there is a debate to be had about whether 'church' as a brand is an appropriate vehicle for attracting people to faith in God. In my former career as a branding consultant, I would remind clients that a brand is what people think about your organization, not necessarily what you say about it. I would start a project with a client by assessing the negative and positive aspects of their current brand and working out with them whether this just needed a tweak or if we should ditch it altogether and do a reset from scratch. In that regard, it cannot be denied that a significant majority of the population do not have a very high opinion of church. Beyond was an initiative to start something that wasn't church, rather than trying to start with a church and evolve it into an arts organization. The church has gone through various major resets in its history: the Reformation is one example, the Franciscan movement is another; maybe it's time for another one?

The work that is described in this book is a serious attempt to help people think deeply about God and the implications these thoughts might have on their own lives, that by creating opportunities for epiphany and letting God work through art, people of faith and people of no faith might experience revelations about God and themselves which can transform them.

When setting out to do this I put together a short presentation about hopes and objectives and showed this to a couple of groups of interested friends and acquaintances. From those meetings the first small team of half a dozen dreamers and activists was formed, but alongside that there was also a team of prayerful supporters, people who didn't feel able to get involved actively in the projects but who did commit themselves to support everything we did in prayer. This was part of the shield to protect us from becoming gimmicky and a check back to make sure that we were being authentic in our desire to reveal God in new ways. I asked three people who I respected as Christian leaders to be our patrons so that I had a group to touch base with every now and then, to make sure we were keeping on track. I also took the concept to groups of local churches and presented it to them, especially to the Anglican Deaneries in Brighton and Hove, so they knew what we were doing and were prepared to assist with publicity and so on.

The people in the team were from a diverse range of churches and faith backgrounds, which helped with spreading the news about the events, and they came with a wide range of skills and passions, which ensured our ideas were very wide ranging. Over the years the personnel in the teams changed, with people dropping out as their life circumstances altered and others joining because they were drawn in by the kinds of things we were doing. We were rarely more than half a dozen active team members, which shows that you don't need a big organization to achieve the kind of work that is described here.

Once all this was in place, I made an application to the Chichester Diocese Mission Fund for a grant to cover running expenses such as venue hire, resource costs, expenditure on publicity and website development. We were awarded a three-year grant for which we were very grateful. That kickstarted the project and we soon developed revenue-generating projects such as a printed Advent Calendar that we could sell as well as being a vehicle for promoting Beyond. We discovered that people love to donate to something that they appreciate and value and so we put out a donation jar every night at the Beach Hut Advent Calendar and the money collected in this way not only paid for the mince pies and drinks but the surplus funded our projects for the rest of the year. We also ran a couple of day conferences on The Art of Ritual and Curating Liturgy that were ticketed; they included an element of training for clergy so could be paid for from church training budgets. In this way, Beyond has been financially self-supporting for 14 years thanks to that initial pump-priming grant.

My life and my faith have been wonderfully enriched by these artistic collaborations and I am privileged to have witnessed people expressing their faith in so many creative ways. There are so many memorable artworks that I haven't had space to write about, including multiple sets of handmade angel wings, animated cardboard models of the nativity, peephole advent calendars, promenade-wide labyrinths of light, giant hut-sized angels, miniature handmade dioramas of the crucifixion, guerrilla performance art in an underground carpark, ice churches dropped into a festival field and 10,000 people joined by ribbons to make a virtual temple.

Being creative has helped me to discover more about our creator God and to have the privilege of seeing others realizing the truth of Genesis 1.26, 'God spoke: "Let us make human beings in our image, make them reflecting our nature"' (*The Message*).